Enough with the

Stuff

something ¢hat u find frustrating)

Strategies for
Defusing Organizational Noise

Dr. Kim D. Kirkland

Acknowledgements

While there are many people and stories that helped shape this publication, I must first and foremost pause and give thanks to my Lord and Savior Jesus Christ, for I have truly been blessed and am thankful for being able to provide you with this body of work that has been coming for some time and is long overdue.

These words aren't mine, particularly "Scuff," which has many origins from Webster and other nationally recognized dictionaries. I used words from our national vocabulary, moved them around or reframed them in a manner that would articulate my story about "Scuff." Thus, this book is not grounded in empirical research, but is more of a common-sense assessment of my perspective of Scuff based on my life's experiences in the field of Equal Employment Opportunity (EEO) compliance and diversity. Hence, this is not an academic book, but an organizational book.

So, here's to you, Pete—all the details and descriptors that I was unable to articulate while serving under your leadership are all so clear to me now. Mr. Peter Knox (Pete), former manager of the Data Center at GE Aviation, aka GE Aircraft Engines, hired me as the manager of Military Products Data Support in 1991. During my four-year tenure under Pete's leadership, I frequently used the term Scuff to describe situations that involved conflict—messy organizational behaviors. Pete would always ask, "Kirkland, what's this Scuff you keep talking about?" Scuff was the only word I could reach for to describe the ills of the folks under my leadership. Some of them were messy, some were gossips, and some were even raggedy, for a lack of a better word, in their approach to interacting with one another. On any given day, this professional group of folks would align divided on many diversity fronts

i

from color—black versus white—gender, education—bachelor's versus high school—military versus non-military, age—under 30 versus over 40—seniority—20+ versus 3-5 years of service, etc. During these trying times as a new leader, I could not quite put my finger on it or articulate it, so Scuff appropriately worked for me. Today, I can say that I am finally able to define it, describe it, and call it out when I see it.

To my current leader, Dr. Charles R. Bantz, executive vice president, Indiana University and chancellor at Indiana University-Purdue University Indianapolis (IUPUI), as well as all the faculty and staff at IUPUI who have embraced the notion of Scuff and affectionately refer to it as such: I can truly say that the use of the term Scuff on the IUPUI campus is a culture re-framing phenomenon.

To Lois Thomas (girlfriend extraordinaire), who did her best to keep this girl on task by making sure that I did not let Scuff get in my own way by keeping my personal commitment to write and stay true to the goal of getting this body of work published.

To Emily Kempski, my administrative assistant, as well as Erin DiBacco, social science research specialist and associate faculty at IUPUI, who both willingly reviewed this body of work for organization, clarity, and structure and provided the much-needed feedback to prepare it for publication—thank you both so much. I am most appreciative of Margo Foreman, senior investigator/assistant director, Diverse Workforce Recruitment and Retention, for literally embracing the notion of Scuff by co-presenting this book with me at various conferences during the past couple years in spite of the book's delayed publication.

I dedicate this body of work to the memory of my late father,
Percy Kirkland, Sr., who was called home on
September 5, 2013 at age 83,
as well as my brother, James William Heard, Jr.,
who received the call much earlier on February 8, 2008 at age 38.
These men had a strong presence in my life and were instru-
mental in shaping this journey. They both gave unconditionally
of themselves, love and support to family, friends, and those
whose lives they touched.
They both leave lifelong footprints on my heart as well as all of
those who knew them.
Both saw something in me I'm not sure I saw in myself.
For that, I will be forever grateful.
Until I see you both again on the other side, continue to
watch over us.
We all loved you and will always miss you both.
As James would most appropriately say "IT IS WHAT IT IS"
AND WHAT THIS IS, IS Scuff
Percy Kirkland, Sr.
August 5, 1930 – September 5, 2013
James William Heard, Jr.
October 1, 1969 – February 8, 2008

Table of Contents

Chapter 1

JUST A LITTLE CONTEXT

Framing It Up

People profess to be annoyed, outraged, aggravated, and angered by just about anything and everything—from how the toilet paper roll is installed, frequent lane changers on the interstate, a slow-moving vehicle in the fast lane, to celebrities' sexual transgressions, to dog-fighting fiascos. People complain about almost anything and everything—from a comment taken out of context, a misinterpreted look, a touch meant in friendship versus companionship, a compliment of appearance that is meant to inspire versus desire, and the like. And, people have filed lawsuits for just about everything from spilled coffee to a person's eligibility to become President of the United States. Americans, in particular, have become the most contentious and litigious culture in the free world.

Recall Stella Liebeck, of Albuquerque, New Mexico, who ordered coffee that was served in a Styrofoam cup at the drive-through window of a McDonald's. After receiving the order, the driver pulled his car forward and stopped so that Liebeck could add cream and sugar to her coffee. Liebeck placed the cup between her knees and attempted to remove the plastic lid from the cup. As she removed the lid, the entire contents of the cup spilled into her lap. The sweatpants Liebeck was wearing absorbed the coffee and held it next to her skin. A vascular surgeon determined that Liebeck suffered full thickness burns (third-degree burns) over 6 percent of her body, including her inner thighs, perineum, buttocks, and groin areas. She was hospitalized for eight days, during which time she underwent skin grafting. Liebeck sued and even though the jury found that she was 20 percent at fault for spilling the coffee, she was awarded compensatory as well as punitive damages for an incident for which she was partially responsible. While public opinion viewed the lawsuit as frivolous before examining Liebeck's injuries, most people now have an understanding of this infamous "Hot Coffee" case (Gwilliam, 2011).

Moreover, recall that Kent (2008) reported that Phillip J. Berg, Esquire, of Pennsylvania filed a lawsuit on behalf of the Democratic Party and citizens of the United States seeking a declaratory judgment and injunction that Barack Obama did not meet the qualifications to become President of the United States. The lawsuit alleged that Obama was not eligible for the presidency because he was not born in the U.S., and/or lost his citizenship when he was adopted in Indonesia, and/or due to his dual citizenship in countries other than the U.S. (Kenya and Indonesia). While some blacks/African-Americans, terms that I may use interchangeably, viewed the lawsuit against President Obama as frivolous as well as racially motivated, past administrations have been taken to task based on their political agenda or other reform issues. For instance, attorney Larry Klayman sued the Bush administration for access to minutes of Vice President Dick Cheney's Energy Task Force.

Public outcry and opinion polls have tested the public's threshold and tolerance over a myriad of issues. The public's outrage over Michael Vick's dog-fighting fiasco landed him in prison. In April 2007, Vick was implicated in an illegal interstate dog-fighting ring that had operated over five years and included hanging, drowning, electrocuting, and shooting dogs. In August 2007, Vick pled guilty to federal felony charges and served twenty-one months in prison, followed by two months of home confinement. After his release, he signed with the Philadelphia Eagles and was reinstated the third week of the 2009 football season. While many Michael Vick supporters who are black allege that the public's outcry and over sensationalized media coverage was based on his race, at the end of the day, Vick was involved in an illegal interstate dog-fighting ring, which is a felony offense. Would there have been the same level of public outcry had Vick been white? We may never know the answer to that question. However, the case drew widespread publicity to the issues of animal abuse and the attention of the Humane Society of the U.S. which is the largest animal advocacy organization in the world.

The public was even more outraged by former Penn State defensive coordinator Gerald "Jerry" Sandusky, who was found guilty of sexual abuse and convicted of forty-five out of forty-eight counts on June 22, 2012. According to Chappell (2012), Sandusky was accused of sexually abusing ten boys over a fifteen-year period in a scandal that rocked the university's community. The allegations against Sandusky ranged from sexual touching to oral and anal sex, and the young men testified they were in their early teens when some of the abuse occurred. There is also evidence that even younger children may have been victimized. While Sandusky maintains his innocence, he says he merely "horsed around" with the boys, all of whom he met through the non-profit Second Mile organization he founded in 1977. Sandusky's scandal cost Penn State University $41 million. At age sixty-eight, Sandusky's thirty- to sixty-year sentence means that he will likely spend the rest of his life in prison.

Unlike many stories about powerful Washington figures having secret affairs, spy chief David Petraeus, who formally oversaw coalition forces in Iraq as well as U.S. and NATO forces in Afghanistan, resigned on November 9, 2012 as head of the CIA after admittedly having an affair with a woman later identified as his biographer, Paula Broadwell. Broadwell, a fellow West Point graduate, spent months studying the general's leadership of U.S. forces in Afghanistan. The affair came to light during an FBI investigation of "jealous" e-mails reportedly sent by Broadwell to a Petraeus family friend. The investigation also prompted questions about whether Broadwell had inappropriate access to classified information.

Former California governor Arnold Schwarzenegger admitted that he fathered a child with Mildred Patricia Baena and hid the secret for sixteen years, shattering his twenty-five-year marriage to Maria Shriver. Baena worked in the family home as a housekeeper and assistant for more than twenty years until her retirement in January 2011. There was a period during his extramarital affair when Baena was working at the couple's Brentwood mansion while pregnant with Schwarzenegger's child at the same time Shriver was pregnant with Schwarzenegger's son Christopher. Schwarzenegger's newly revealed child and Christopher were born less than a week apart.

I would be remiss not to give a notable mention to the top sports story that exploded in late November 2009 and rolled into 2010 until the BP oil spill took center stage: the continued insistence that world-renowned professional golfer Tiger Woods' sexual transgressions be examined in the public. After the story broke, many people became extremely angry over the fact that Tiger Woods had extramarital affairs with not only one woman, but more than a dozen women. Again, black people in my particular circles viewed the intensity and severity of the media hype as an attempt to bring another celebrated black man to his knees and put him in his place. While Woods refers to himself as Cablinasian (Caucasian, Black, American Indian, and Asian), many black people embrace him as a black man. Meanwhile, the office water cooler chatter, Twitter, and blogs indicate that many people personalized the revelation of Woods' sexual transgressions. As the story unfolded, some people commented that they were annoyed, that the situation got on their nerves, and that it made them sick to the point where some wanted his balls (literally) on a silver platter for what he did to his wife. The public was adamant that Woods apologize, hold a press conference, speak publicly about his behaviors, and the like.

While some blacks contend that the Tiger Woods scandal received a lot more coverage than Schwarzenegger and Petraeus, was it racially motivated or did the sheer volume of women involved in Woods' scandal have more to do with the media coverage? The fact that women were stepping forward almost on a daily basis, admitting to having an affair with Tiger Woods, may explain why the story virtually took on a life of its own and was up way past its bedtime. I am also of the opinion that the manner in which the transgressions were played out in the media had more to do with their celebrity status than any personal characteristic related to their race or ethnicity. Had these incidents involved a regular Joe, no one would have cared except for the people directly involved.

Again, Michael Vick was involved in an illegal interstate dog-fighting ring, which is a felony offense. Tiger Woods made an informed adult decision to step out of his relationship and cheat on his wife despite the consequences for his actions and got caught. And President Obama, unfortunately, holds the most powerful and prestigious position in the United States of America, making him an easy target for criticism, and he is always under scrutiny. Unlike with Vick, Woods, and President Obama, white people never ventured to play the race card or attempted to imply Sandusky, Schwarzenegger, or Petraeus' downfalls were predicated on their race, but their behaviors.

Americans will openly espouse their opinion through the critique of everything from political affiliation to the disrespect of our nation's first black President, Barack Obama. And, while it may appear that black people allege transgressions based on race more than other races, not everything that happens to black people is actually grounded in race, or at least it most often cannot be proven. While President Obama, Michael Vick, and Tiger Woods are all men of color, the specific incidents described herein were not necessarily attributed to their color, nor were they the result of their race.

Americans tend to hold people accountable for what happens in their personal life as well as what happens in their professional life, particularly when they are a celebrity or public figure. Moreover, people will take a position on or express an opinion on just about anything and every issue from a personal, professional, social, or political perspective. Accordingly, people will take individuals or institutions to task as they deem appropriate or necessary because in most situations they have nothing to lose by doing so.

While not every public or personal transgression or misdeed is without impunity, harm, or recrimination, Scuff can happen to people simply because of the position or title they hold as with President Obama. Sometimes it is a result of people's own reckless and irresponsible behaviors as with Vick and Sandusky. And sometimes it comes from personal actions that are self-induced as with Woods, Schwarzenegger, and Petraeus. In other situations, Scuff can simply occur because of an unintentional cultural misstep on someone's part or a failure to communicate, which may be grounded in culture. Even in situations involving cultural missteps or miscommunications, people should not be so quick to reach for race, age, gender, religion, sexual orientation, or other characteristic as the basis of the affront.

Like issues brought to light in the public arena or media, workplace issues take on a similar level of transparency and accountability. Employees in private or corporate organizations, government, higher education, and nonprofit institutions alike will complain about almost any and everything. While organizations may not experience the same level of outrage, outcry, or opinion polls that are played out in the media or broader society, employees expect recourse based on the ideology of accountability. What that translates to in the workplace are union protests, strikes or walkouts, climate surveys, and employee complaints through internal processes, external agencies such as the EEOC and the OCR, or federal lawsuits.

Many employees are offended, annoyed, or bothered by a spoken word of compliment (you look nice today); by open-air water cooler conversations about religion, politics, sexual orientation, or the like; by a display of horseplay that is personally perceived as inappropriate; by an unwelcome touch on the shoulder, arm, or back area; by any cultural transgression intentional or not (an insensitive stray remark related to one's personal characteristic); and the like. Even some of the smallest infractions and annoyances create anxiety in some employees. While most of these issues that are raised in the workplace are framed as harassment or discrimination, what most likely is occurring is organizational noise—a miscommunication or misunderstanding potentially grounded in culture between the parties because people no longer talk to one another. Instead people will raise issues with someone they expect to go and straighten someone else out for resolution, or they send an inappropriate text or email message in response.

A lot of age-old dysfunctional behaviors and actions are recurring in organizations that may blur the lines of illegal harassment and/or discrimination. Historically, these behaviors have carried many different labels such as mistake, mishap, miscommunication, misunderstanding, or even a cultural misstep. However, more recently, new labels have been added to this montage of behaviors that now includes insults, infractions, micro-inequities, bullying, and mobbing *(See Appendix A – Glossary of Terms)*.

This book will journey into the messy mislabels, missteps, mishaps, misunderstandings, and miscommunications of social and organizational behavior. I use the terms "social" and "organizational" because people will bring issues from their personal life and/or community into the workplace for resolution, particularly if an amorous relationship occurred that went bad and they both happen to work for the same organization. Unfortunately, their issues get played out in the organization and someone has to fix it. Yes, we become the "gladiators." We fix this S*cu*ff. Anybody who watches the popular television series *Scandal* and is familiar with the leading character Olivia Pope and her team knows exactly what I'm talking about. We fix people's mishaps, missteps, misunderstandings, and miscommunications because they cannot, will not, or are just unable to manage the situation themselves.

Moreover, this book gives organizational professionals permission to fondly reach for the term S*cu*ff when identifying and addressing organizational noise versus reaching for the traditional trappings of mislabeling the behaviors or actions as harassment and discrimination. Lastly, this book will provide organizations with formal and informal strategies for addressing the S*cu*ff.

Chapter 2

WHAT IS IT?

Toilet Paper Roll

Allow me to digress here and tell you a story about a small personal annoyance that bothers most people—the position in which the toilet paper roll is installed (the "over" position versus the "under" position). While I personally prefer that the roll be installed in the "under" position, I recall a time when sitting in my sister's bathroom in their home and putting in a little paperwork. Now mind you, in my personal bathroom, I have stuff to do (read a magazine or book, browse through shopping catalogues, etc.). I had nothing to do in my sister's bathroom, so as I sat there with a little time on my hands, I took a visual tour of my surroundings and noticed that the toilet paper roll was installed the wrong way in the "over" position. The longer I sat there looking at the roll, the more I became annoyed with the fact that she

The Toilet Paper Roll

The right way   The wrong way

or someone in the household had installed the toilet paper roll the wrong way. I must say that I took the liberty of releasing the roll from the holder and reinstalling the toilet paper roll in the right position—the "under" position.

Go figure—in that short period of time, I decided that the right way to install a roll of toilet paper was my way, which is in the "under" position. While it has been more than thirty years since my sister and I have shared the same living space, imagine how this small nuisance could surmount if we occupied the same space on a daily basis. One possible scenario is that this could possibly drive me totally batty and get on my last nerve to the point where we would possibly begin debating and/or arguing over the position in which a toilet paper roll should be installed. Please believe me when I tell you that I actually know there is no right or wrong way in which to install a roll of toilet paper—the roll is installed based on one's personal preference, habit, i.e., the manner in which one has become accustomed to installing it.

Remember the phrase "don't sweat the small Stuff?" Well, this is some of that small Stuff that can frustrate folks, get on their nerves, or make them "sick" to the point where they want to see a change in behavior or outcome. Meaning, they want to see the toilet paper roll installed the "right" way, which is their way. The good news is that I recently saw a television commercial advertising a toilet paper roll that can flip in either the "under" or the "over" position, which would accommodate everybody— problem solved. While I have yet to see this product on the shelves in any of the giant superstores, such a commodity would take every household in America by storm due to its versatility.

Some people profess that similar small infractions get on their nerves or make them sick; people profess to be sick and tired of a situation, and everybody knows that tired always follows sick; and people will finally profess that they just can't take it anymore.

Now, without conducting a formal survey and without doing

any research or performing any type of statistical analysis, I can say for a fact that most "baby boomers" and "matures" are sick and tired of seeing our young men walk around with their pants sagging. While this example may be generational, it doesn't take a rocket scientist to know some S*uff or at least figure it out. Although some professional sports athletes and other celebrity role models have suited up (shirt and tie), the behavior has yet to be modeled on a large scale.

Let's look at a small infraction in the classroom. A guy leaned back in his chair and stretched in a manner that extended his arms over his head and exposed his stomach, as he was wearing a T-shirt. A female student was offended by the incident and alleged sexual harassment. Just because someone is annoyed, upset, or aggravated by another person's action or behavior— or something gets on a person's nerve or makes them "sick"—it does not mean that the issue is legitimately grounded in sexual harassment or discrimination. However, people will want even the smallest of infractions and annoyances stopped.

While my story above began at the level of a roll of toilet paper, in the workplace, once an employee begins seeking an external resource for resolution of their issues and concerns outside of the organization, they view their issue(s) to be far beyond that of the toilet paper roll. Valid or not, it is the employee's perspective. In organizations, many employees tend to wrap the S*uff that happens to them, not around the toilet paper roll, but around their race, age, gender, disability, religion, national origin, sexual orientation, or other protected characteristic that garners an official review for disparate treatment from an equal opportunity perspective. In most situations, such small infractions or annoyances in the workplace like the one above are not actually grounded in illegal harassment or illegal discrimination; it's just S*uff. However, it's the S*uff that is getting on people's nerves, making them sick, and they want it officially stopped.

Stuff Defined

The term Stuff is used in many contexts and has become the catchphrase for just about everything, from what we have (objects and possessions) to what we do (work, errands, activities) to some of the most unfortunate situations we have found ourselves in. Incidents that have happened to us have also been referred to as Stuff that happens.

Based on Collins (2013) World English Dictionary, stuff can be used as a noun or a verb. When used as a verb, stuff requires action such as cram something into a cavity (the child stuffed candy into his pockets); press or force (stuff money into an envelope); block or obstruct (my nose is all stuffed); gorge, overindulge, overeat, binge, pig out (she stuffed herself at dinner); and force or stuff (fill with a stuffing, stuff a bearskin, or stuff a pillow with feathers).

As a noun, stuff can be described as the tangible substance that goes into the makeup of a physical object (wheat is the stuff they use to make bread); miscellaneous unspecified objects (the trunk was full of stuff); informal terms for personal possessions (did you take all your stuff or clobber?); nonsense, poppycock, and senseless talk (don't give me that stuff); unspecified qualities required to do or be something (you don't have the stuff to be a United States Marine); and information in some unspecified form (it was stuff I had heard before or there's good stuff in this book).

The essence of stuff comes in all shapes, forms, sizes, and ideas of what stuff is, and it is referred to from both a concrete and an abstract perspective. From a concrete perspective stuff is solid, real, specific, tangible, particular, actual, distinct, definite, material, and physical—it can be seen and is able to be touched because it exists in reality, not just as an idea. For example, people buy stuff and store it in their closets, their homes are full of stuff, they store extra stuff in the garage, every drawer in their kitchen is filled with a multitude of stuff, practically every woman carries more stuff in her handbag than the law should allow, and when people run out of places to put the stuff they currently have, they go buy more stuff to store that stuff.

From an abstract perspective, stuff is theoretical, conceptual, intangible, nonfigurative, nonrepresentational, extract, précis, or a synopsis—not relating to concrete objects but expressing something that can only be appreciated intellectually or based on general principles or theories rather than on specific instances. It is at times said that some people sure know their stuff, and the stuff they know is some good stuff. People often comment that they have stuff to do. What this means is they have activities, errands, or engagements to attend. People also have a tendency to comment that a whole bunch of stuff just happened—incidents, situations, etc. We know stuff, we have stuff to do, and stuff happens—enough with the Stuff.

Stuff—Something That U Find Frustrating

In the context of this book, the Stuff that we will be referring to is "Something That U Find Frustrating"—it's the stuff that gets on people's nerves, it's the stuff that makes people angry, it's the stuff people don't like—it's distracting and disruptive to people's daily psyche, and some say it's the stuff that makes them sick. The Stuff we're talking about here is NOT *illegal harassment,* which is behavior that threatens or torments somebody, especially persistently but also includes inappropriate practices and behaviors such as jokes or disparaging remarks. NOR is it *illegal discrimination,* which occurs by treating people differently through prejudice on the basis of their race, color, religion, national origin, sex, age, pregnancy, disability, veteran status, or genetic information.

More broadly, *harassment* is a form of employment discrimination. Harassment is unwelcome conduct that is based on race, color, religion, sex (including pregnancy), national origin, age (forty or older), disability, or genetic information. Harassment becomes unlawful where 1) enduring the offensive conduct becomes a condition of continued employment, or 2) the conduct is severe or pervasive enough to create a work environment that a reasonable person would consider intimidating, hostile, or abusive. For example, it is illegal to harass a woman by making offensive comments about women in general. Other types of harassment include inappropriate practices and behaviors such as jokes or disparaging remarks that might be funny to one person, but offensive to another. Some people do not even realize that what they say is offensive to those around them. It's a ripple effect when someone hears someone say something they don't know is wrong, but they think it is "cool" or "hip," so they use it somewhere else. Eventually someone is offended by what's said.

Although the law doesn't prohibit simple teasing, offhand comments, or isolated incidents that are not very serious, consequently petty slights, annoyances, and isolated incidents (unless extremely serious) will not rise to the level of illegality. Harassment is illegal when it is so frequent or severe that it creates a hostile or offensive work environment or when it results in an adverse employment decision (such as the victim being fired or demoted). Offensive conduct may include, but is not limited to, offensive jokes, slurs, epithets, or name calling, physical assaults or threats, intimidation, ridicule, or mockery, insults or put-downs, offensive objects or pictures, and interference with work performance. Moreover, the harasser can be the victim's supervisor, a supervisor in another area, a coworker, or a non-employee such as a client or customer. The victim does not have to be the person harassed, but can be anyone affected by the offensive conduct.

Discrimination consists of treating individuals or specific groups of people differently. It is illegal to discriminate against someone on the basis of race, color, religion, national origin, sex, age, pregnancy, disability, veteran status, or genetic information. The law also requires that employers reasonably accommodate applicants' and employees' sincerely held religious practices, unless doing so would impose an undue hardship on the operation of the employer's business. Anti-discrimination laws also prohibit harassment against individuals in retaliation for filing a discrimination charge, testifying, or participating in any way in an investigation, proceeding, or lawsuit under these laws; or opposing employment practices that they reasonably believe discriminate against individuals, in violation of these laws.

By no means am I attempting to mitigate the seriousness of relevant or bona-fide complaints of harassment or discrimination filed in the workplace based on protected characteristics. Rather, I am merely attempting to provide clarity around some small annoyances that are perceived to be harassment or discrimination or that have a tendency to get mislabeled as harassment or discrimination.

Let's reframe an earlier example and say that a female instructor raised an allegation of sexual harassment because a male student sitting in class stretched—as he raised his hands over his head, his T-shirt lifted, exposing his belly. The female instructor was so offended and distraught that she left class and went home for the remainder of the day. Was this incident sexual harassment?

The behavior in this scenario does not rise to a level of sexual harassment as alleged—it was Scuff—something that she found frustrating. Was it intentional?—Probably not. However, the female instructor would argue that the incident got on her nerves, that she found it annoying and most arguably offensive. While many people will have an opinion about whether the incident was offensive or whether it was sexual harassment, in the context of where and how the incident occurred, it was not sexual harassment. This was an isolated incident that was not very serious, frequent, or so severe that it would pass the reasonable person's test in creating a hostile or offensive work environment. This is the type of Scuff I'm talking about. Take a look at my use of the spelling of the word Scuff. It looks messy—actually it appears as if it's misspelled. That is because the Scuff that is raised on a large scale in most organizations is generally messy, perceived as petty, most probably a conflict between two parties that resulted from a misunderstanding, a mishap, or a failure to communicate. Scuff at times, has even been perceived as a micro-inequity, which is a subtle message, sometimes subconscious, that devalues, discourages, and ultimately impairs performance in the workplace. These messages can take the shape of looks, gestures, or even tones. The cumulative effect of micro-inequities often leads to damaged self-esteem and, eventually, withdrawal from coworkers in the office. If employees could chalk up their incidents to a simple misunderstanding and move on, they would, though most can't. To use an art analogy in which pictures are matted, then framed to project the best perspective—employees mat their issues, then come back and frame those issues up as harassment or discrimination based on one or more of the protected characteristics in order to get an official review from the appropriate internal (Equal Opportunity, Affirmative Action, Human Resources) or external (EEOC or OCR) authority.

Some employees like playing in the dirt (messy mishaps)—some even feel the need to add water and stir because they like the situation muddy and messy. These types of employees are referred to as "pot stirrers" or "troublemakers" because they won't allow a situation to mend itself or simmer down. They like the flames turned up high on the front burner in the organization for everyone to see. Most of us know who the "pot stirrers" are. The messy behaviors these people produce become the Scuff that gets on people's nerves and makes them sick, because the behaviors have a tendency to get out of hand and contaminate others. By whatever means Scuff gets raised or finds its way into the light of day, it has a tendency to wreak havoc in an organization if left without redress. Employees will stew on their issues until they get resolution; they will create allies sympathetic to their plight; and/or they will shop their issue(s) across the organization until they get an outcome they are satisfied with or can live with. You best believe that they won't go away until the issue(s) does.

How Stuff Happens—The Boiling Point

Have you ever been in the presence of someone who insists on having an open-air cell phone conversation among strangers? Well, a little while ago I visited the dealership to have my car serviced. Within five minutes of my arrival into the waiting area, another customer I'll call "Kathy" proceeded to hold an open-air cell phone conversation amid this somewhat crowded space. This waiting space in the showroom was equipped with a flat-screen TV, a child's play area, coffee service, water bottle service, laptop hook-ups, Internet access via Wi-Fi, and seven chairs, five of which were taken. There were four other people besides Kathy in this small space, and she was so loud that anyone passing by would have thought the television was temporarily placed on mute because you couldn't hear it over her cell phone conversation.

Shortly after I made myself a cup of coffee and took a seat, Kathy's phone rang. She acknowledged the caller, and based on her reaction to the information being communicated to her, you would have thought someone had died. In a dramatic manner Kathy responded to the caller by saying, "Oh my God, what happened?" Her expressed emotion led me to look at her, waiting for a waterfall of tears that never came. After a few moments of silence, she said, "Well, why on earth would they cancel your classes? What will you do for the next three hours? Did you bring something to work on?" I knew then that the four of us would be held hostage and trapped into viewing a stage play for which we had not purchased tickets, a show starring Kathy as the "drama queen" for a performance that was just shy of an Oscar nod. She had no consideration for the people around her and was totally oblivious to the fact that four other people were working on their laptop, reading the newspaper, or trying to watch the breaking news broadcast/updates about the election of the new Pope. It was apparent that the caller must have asked what else Kathy had going on for the day, as she responded, "Well, I probably won't make it to my book club meeting or either I'll be late. But I can't go anywhere looking like this. I look a mess. I have on the same clothes from yesterday from when I was at my niece's house. She has two little ones so I have two rounds of throw-up on these clothes, but I decided to wear this over here this morning."

Now mind you, as she uttered the word "throw-up," I turned to assess her attire out of the corner of my eye and caught the woman across from me looking over her glasses to likewise assess what two rounds of throw-up on this outfit looked like.

The customer service rep approached Kathy to inform her that she needed some additional repair work, and Kathy immediately informed the caller that she would call right back. After a short discussion, she instructed the customer service rep to proceed with the additional repairs because she was scheduled to leave town the next day. So, sad to say, she immediately returned the call and picked up right where she had left off.

By now, unsurprisingly, Kathy was getting on everyone's nerves, but no one had the courage to tell her that she was being rude and insensitive or to ask her to dial the volume on her call down a notch. I intentionally decided against being the spokesperson for our small cohort since I was the only person of color in the room. I made a decision not to be perceived as the angry black woman with too much attitude. While my role at work requires that I address and/or take people on for bad or inappropriate behaviors that are counter to the organization's policies, I decided not to don my compliance hat in this situation or to police Kathy's behavior even if it would be for the greater good.

So, Kathy's conversation resumed in traditional *Seinfeld* fashion about absolutely nothing—the traffic, the weather, her trip tomorrow, how she loved and missed the caller, a reiteration that she was wearing the same clothes from the day before that she had worn to her niece's house, and yada, yada, yada. After what felt like an hour but was more like ten minutes later, Kathy informed the caller that it would be at least another hour and a half before her car would be ready. Based on Kathy's response the caller must have asked if she needed a ride, to which Kathy responded—"I'll wait, it's too far for you to come get me, blah, blah, blah, maybe they can give me a ride home"—at which time a smile crossed my face at the thought of Kathy leaving.

By now, this Scuff was working my last nerve. Scuff in this scenario was Kathy's invasive cell phone conversation, at least as I was experiencing it, which was invading other people's space, mine in particular. When Kathy stepped out of the waiting room to ask for a ride home, my wish was granted. Imagine the relief I felt as I anticipated being rid of this annoying woman. When Kathy walked out the door, I wanted to ask, "Does anyone hear that?"—"What?" the others would ask. "Silence," I would reply with a long, deep sigh. She was gone. I immediately took pen to paper so as not to lose the playback of this messy moment of the Scuff my cohorts and I found frustrating. While I believe that deep down inside, all of us wanted to stand up and cheer as Kathy exited stage left, we instead suffered in silence and stewed on this Scuff. I clearly resented her behavior because not only did I capture this mid-morning matinee with pen and paper, I decided it was annoying enough to include here as an excellent example of the Scuff that I found frustrating, because it literally got on my nerves as it appeared to for everyone else.

Any one of us could have said, "Excuse me, would you mind taking your conversation out into the lobby? Some of us are trying to work or watch television and can't do that at the current volume in which you are holding your conversation," or some words to that effect. While some of us may have reached our boiling point with Kathy, we all sat in silence and stewed on this S𝑐uff.

Kathy's off-Broadway performance occurred outside the workplace among strangers, but this type of obsessive need to be immediately accessible has an impact in many settings. Imagine how a similar scenario would play out in the workplace where colleagues are more intimately familiar with one another. In such an instance, the open-air conversation could even be a little more offensive in subject, tone, and/or language. These small annoyances can mount up and are sometimes compounded by a progressive buildup of separate incidents that ultimately take on a life bigger than the original incident. At the end of the day, this accumulation of S𝑐uff can translate into serious transgressions against the recipient.

Imagine that if such a small infraction, annoyance, or nuisance like an open-air cell phone conversation can violate the personal space of four strangers in a waiting area, what in the world is happening with employees in their workplace space with similar or other issues in which there is more of an emotional connection to the people who annoy them? Colleagues are not just passing strangers. The smallest of these infractions that I refer to as S𝑐uff are wreaking havoc in most organizations today more than ever. There could be a number of reasons why this is happening more frequently. With organizations moving toward business casual attire, people may have lost the ability to be formal and professional; or in the age of technology people are less attuned to other people's feelings; or the "bitchy" Hollywood portrayals and the phenomena of bad behavior being played out on reality TV shows make rudeness acceptable; or maybe parents are raising oblivious, self-centered adults.

Employees engage in petty bickering, some not so petty, and communication is lacking because people don't talk to one another anymore—they stew over or sit on these issues, or hold onto this S𝑐uff until they reach their boiling point. The boiling point is that pivotal point at which people lose their tempers because the situation has become intolerable or critical—to where Scuff is frustrating folks, Scuff is getting on people's nerves, Scuff is making people sick, and they want the behaviors or actions stopped or fixed. Again, once an employee seeks resolution from an external resource outside the organization, they are way beyond issues at the level of the toilet paper roll. And while most small infractions in the workplace are not necessarily illegal harassment or illegal discrimination, it is still Scuff that the employees want stopped.

Before conflicting, unpleasant, or frustrating workplace issues bring an employee to their boiling point, it is always the organization's hope that they will first seek out internal resources such as the organization's Office of Equal Opportunity or Affirmative Action Office, ombudsperson, diversity office, human resources office, or their immediate supervisor, if appropriate. In institutions of higher education, faculty members can also seek resolution from an internal governing review board to address academic-related issues or to help navigate their Scuff. Students can seek assistance from a student advocate, ombudsperson, advisor or someone in the Student Life or Student Affairs organization to help facilitate resolution or navigate their Scuff.

In any case, staff, faculty, and students will not hesitate to pursue external resources or to "lawyer up" if they believe they have been treated unfairly (harassment, discrimination, retaliation, or improperly accommodated). Even if an employee's issue(s) has been determined by appropriate authorities to be Scuff versus illegal harassment or discrimination, they may also seek resolution from an investigatory enforcement agency such as the governmental Equal Employment Opportunity Commission (EEOC) or the Office of Civil Rights (OCR) when they believe the organization has either let them down or will be ineffective in addressing what they assert are issues in the workplace based on some protected status (race, sex, color, national origin,

ancestry, age, religion, disability, orientation, veteran status).
In many instances, employees will shop their issues simultaneously throughout and across the organization as well as with an external agency, using every available resource until they get the outcome they are seeking—someone in authority saying they were adversely treated or righteously offended by something. Someone in authority who can then go and straighten someone out or fix the situation.

Enforcement Agencies

What follows is some relevant context to describe the three primary agencies responsible for enforcing federal laws that prohibit employment discrimination, discrimination in all programs or activities that receive federal financial assistance and require federal contractors and subcontractors to take affirmative action to ensure that all individuals have an equal opportunity for employment, without regard to race, color, religion, sex, national origin, disability, or veteran status.

A link to each of these agencies can be found in **Appendix B**, but the critical details for this discussion are as follows:

1. *The U.S. Equal Employment Opportunity Commission (EEOC)* enforces federal laws prohibiting employment discrimination that involves unfair treatment because of your **race, color, religion, sex (including pregnancy), national origin, disability,** or **age** (age forty or older); harassment by managers, coworkers, or others in the workplace, based on race, color, religion, sex (including pregnancy), national origin, disability, or age; denial of a reasonable workplace accommodation for religious beliefs or disability; or retaliation because you complained about job discrimination, or assisted with a job discrimination investigation or lawsuit.

2. *The Office for Civil Rights (OCR)* ensures equal access to education and promotes educational excellence through vigorous enforcement of civil rights. An important responsibility is resolving complaints of discrimination on behalf of student populations.

3. *The Office of Federal Contract Compliance Programs (OFCCP)* is responsible for ensuring that contractors doing business with the federal government do not discriminate and do take affirmative action.

These agencies enforce federal laws prohibiting discrimination and require federal contractors and subcontractors to take affirmative action to ensure that all individuals have an equal opportunity for employment, without regard to race, color, religion, sex, age, national origin, disability, or status as a Vietnam-era or special disabled veteran.

Unfortunately, oftentimes the staff employees complain about to agencies has a tendency to get mislabeled due to a cultural misstep by a colleague, a misunderstanding between conflicting parties, or a fumbled communication exchange between parties that was poorly mishandled by a supervisor or manager. Sometimes people just don't know what they don't know, and sometimes people are culturally ignorant and clueless to the fact that their behavior(s) may be viewed as insensitive or offensive, or misperceived by a receiving party. If we're ever going to bridge this diversity divide, employees need to be given the tools to try communication exchanges that permit dialogue and understanding of other's cultures and backgrounds before escalating to finger pointing and blame through assertions of harassment or discrimination. In other words, people just need to talk to each other.

When I use the term "mislabeled," I am referring to issues that employees file with an agency (EEOC or OCR) under the pretext of harassment, discrimination, or retaliation, which are really S*uff. Oftentimes employees know their issue(s) is not based on any protected characteristic, but will wrap their complaints around one of the characteristics that falls under the jurisdiction of a particular agency in order to get a formal review. And more often than not, the underlying issue is S*uff grounded in the conflicting parties' inability to communicate, a misunderstanding that may also be due to a failure to communicate, or a misstep in which the complaining party's cultural toes were stepped on, offending, insulting, emotionally hurting, or frustrating the complaining party. Regardless of the incident, the complaining party wants some behavior stopped, fixed, changed, eliminated or someone fired. And, in most situations the complaining party is unable or unwilling to communicate their displeasure with the insult or infraction to the responding party and is consequently left to seek solace in an agency when they do not get the outcome they are seeking internally.

When an organization receives notice that an employee or student has filed a charge with an agency, the unit or department directly connected to the charge is quick to refute any wrongdoing. They may even take it as a personal affront to their integrity and character because someone has accused them of an unlawful act. Nobody enjoys being accused of being racist or sexist or having discriminated against or harassed someone.

Chapter 3

WHAT IS THIS STUFF ALL ABOUT?

The Beginning of Stuff for Me

I begin this chapter by sharing my personal best and worst story around the messy mishaps of organizational behavior. It began in the early 1990s during my first big leadership role in a Fortune 500 manufacturing company in the Midwest. The team of twenty-four staff members included seven white men, four black men, eight white women, and five black women. I can take no credit for this diversity, although I applaud the efforts of my predecessor, who had the determination and courage to hold the organization accountable for their espoused commitment to diversity.

In addition to its racial and gender diversity, 35 percent of the team had been in the organization ten or more years, while the others had less than three years' seniority. Almost all of the relatively recent hires held a bachelor's degree and were in their mid- to late twenties. The more senior individuals were all over forty and did not have a college degree; although most of the men were Vietnam-era veterans with "military degrees" as were the customary reference.

Almost as soon as I arrived, the organizational noise was turned up on blast as employees had been stewing on past unresolved conflicts and issues which began to split the team and impair their ability to operate as a cohesive unit. These issues ranged from military experience versus non-military experience, college degree versus high school degree, young versus mature, as well as black versus white. This group of folks would split on just about all these dimensions of diversity depending on the issue on any given day. While I don't profess to have invented the word Scuff, it became a permanent staple of my vocabulary during my tenure in this organization, as it most accurately defined for me the absence of any real compliance issues regarding harassment or discrimination, though these folks were quick to reach for them for just about any situation.

I was a new and relatively young leader, and issues were cropping up left and right. I don't know how well this team got along prior to my arrival, but after I started there, the office turned into an elementary school playground—folks couldn't get along, everything that was said or done became an issue, arguments became the mainstay, and accusations of favoritism, racism, and discrimination resounded around the water cooler. I was no longer managing the work and providing leadership because the Scuff had taken on a life of its own—completely taken over. I spoke with my manager regarding some of these dynamics that I surmised had been festering for some time because folks had never had an opportunity to talk through their issues with one another. When I showed up pushing the concept of teams, I also had the nerve to restructure the organization around that concept—WOW—yeah, that's right—WOW. As I attempted to explain the situation from my perspective to my manager, I constantly referred to these messy mishaps as Scuff. Now, my manager was an information technology (IT) guy, so he pressed me to define what this Scuff was. He'd ask, "Kirkland—what's this Scuff you keep talking about?" The best way I could describe Scuff was by reciting the individual scenarios of the many incidents that mirrored what I'd also call high school behavior. Then, I would end the explanation by saying something like "It's just Scuff. During that time, I could not articulate a label that would appropriately describe these messy mishaps and issues. All I could do was bundle the issues as Scuff for lack of a better term.

Well, let me tell you this— Scuff can make or break you and it was working on this girl's last nerve. This Scuff was so exhausting, I decided that I had had enough and was ready to say "when." It was time to address the Scuff that kept my group from working as three effective self-directed work teams.

Now, if you were to think that was the end of my Scuff and it was all uphill from there, you would be wrong. However, I was thinking nothing more could happen as I was already dealing with a myriad of Scuff. In the midst of the change initiative to a team-based approach, the tension in the group erupted and divided the group into racial pockets when a black woman (Carla) confronted a white woman (Theresa) about negative remarks she was rumored to have made about her to her customers. While Carla accused Theresa of exaggerating the incident with an over-dramatized display of tears several hours after the confrontation, Theresa insisted that Carla blocked her path in a hostile and threatening manner. Visibly shaken by the confrontation, real or not, Theresa filed a formal complaint of "Violence in the Workplace" against Carla because she perceived the incident to be physically threatening. I personally conducted an investigation, but collaborated and consulted with the unit's Human Relations manager during the process. As a result of findings from the investigation, Carla received an oral and written reprimand. Theresa, having viewed the incident as more severe, felt that Carla should have been terminated. As a result, Theresa began overtly aligning other white members of the team against Carla, further inflaming racial tensions and creating more opposition to the team-based initiative.

Transitioning the group to a team-based approach amid this turmoil now presented a dual challenge. In response to these challenges, I took the following critical actions to ensure continued progress toward the team-based approach and to address the personnel conflicts:

1. Appointed team leaders who the group members respected and who were knowledgeable about the products, the systems, as well as the customers.
2. Empowered the teams to make decisions regarding their work processes. For example, an employee requested a change in her work schedule to address child care issues. Pushing the request back to the team for approval enabled action on their part and negated the appearance of special treatment.
3. Attended weekly meetings with each work team to create a shared vision about the value of teamwork and the impact on productivity, to gauge the pulse of the team members, to identify resource requirements, and to address issues and concerns as they arose.
4. Provided training opportunities that were essential to retooling outdated technical and soft skills.
5. Sponsored an all-day *mandatory* sensing session that was facilitated by an Employee Assistance Program consultant and included the entire team, my direct reporting manager, and the HR manager. The purpose of the sensing session was to provide the team members with an opportunity to express their feelings about the team-based initiative, to begin healing old wounds that had manifested themselves over the years, to address the recent exit of a colleague at that time, as well as to address the racial tension that had resulted from the Carla-Theresa fiasco.

As the leader, my challenge was to make sense of these messy mishaps in an effort to find some basis and enough support for reasonable and supported action to occur (Sergiovanni, Kellerher, McCarthy, and Wirt, 2004). In hindsight, more compassion and sensitivity to Theresa's feelings regarding the incident with Carla could have resulted in a different response from her. For example, coaching could have validated her value to the team and the organization as well as curtailed the energy she spent recruiting followers. According to Sergiovanni, Kellerher, McCarthy, and Wirt (2004), conflict is natural and is to be expected in dynamic organizations, it is not abnormal, nor is it necessarily a symptom of a breakdown in an organization's community. Organizations are fragmented into many power blocks and self-directed interest groups; therefore, it is natural that these power blocs and interest groups will try to influence policy so that their values and goals are given priority and consideration.

Hence, Theresa was using her power base to influence the team's response to the team-based initiative as well as their perception of Carla. Theresa was a long-service employee, politically savvy and well connected across the organization. Possibly a broader role that accentuated her customer relations skills could have kept her as the ally she initially professed to be rather than the enemy that she later viewed herself to be. It is behaviors such as these that culminated in my use of the term S*cuff*.

Unfortunately, no amount of venting, acting out, or sensing sessions would enable Theresa to heal the emotional scars she felt were left from the incident with Carla, as she was now operating on sheer hate alone. As I stated earlier, if employees could chalk up their incident to a simple misunderstanding and move on, they would. In this situation, Theresa could not move on—she did not just try the conflict on, she was wearing it and had buttoned and zipped it up. She liked it messy—she liked playing in the dirt and would add water and stir on a daily basis through the recruitment of other team members and allies sympathetic to her plight regarding Carla. Theresa cultivated the continued water cooler chatter and flame-fanning of the incident. But more importantly, her actions continued to bridge a broader racial divide within the unit. Theresa's behavior could clearly be described as "pot stirring," as she would not allow the situation to mend itself or simmer down, even after the sensing session in which everyone agreed that the matter related to her and Carla was closed and we would move forward as a team. Theresa kept the flames turned up high on the front burner in the organization for everyone to see, and those flames continued to wreak havoc on productivity.

Eventually, Theresa left me no choice but to address her behavior in her annual performance appraisal; she was unreachable through verbal communication and would not put past events behind her. She would not let go of the fact that Carla was not terminated for an incident that she helped cultivate and could not see the role she had played in instigating the confrontation. Putting Theresa on notice in this manner sent a message to her loyal cohorts who were also continuing to fan the flames of the past. Though subtle, the message that Theresa was on her way out if her behavior did not change was apparent. Team members knew that some form of discipline, including discharge, was possible because they had witnessed the exit of another team member earlier in my tenure.

While Theresa found Carla's behavior threatening, what she found frustrating was the fact that Carla was not terminated for the behavior. And while Theresa did not get the outcome she was looking for or view that the incident was resolved to her satisfaction, Carla's behavior and actions were addressed. Unfortunately, I found myself at a crossroads with Theresa's behavior, and it was time to deal with her Scuff. According to Sergiovanni, Kellerher, McCarthy, and Wirt (2004), "Decision making is constrained by the inability of people to account for and use all the available information that under optimal conditions would produce a maximum decision." Allowing Theresa's disruptive behavior to continue would have been counterproductive to the greater good of the team goals and could not be tolerated any longer. I was forced to set the standard of acceptable behavior and was not prepared to continue dealing with Theresa's Stuff. While this journey had its share of roadblocks, was mentally and emotionally taxing as well as stressful, the upshot was highly productive, self-directed work teams. This experience exposed the many facets of my character, strengthened my communication skills, provided an array of technical abilities, and helped to shape me as a leader. This experience is recorded in my repertoire as a personal best and worst. I was forced to make some tough decisions in the face of popularity, and the challenges were endless. Ultimately, in an economic downturn I presented employees with severance packages as a result of business-wide workforce reductions; reorganized the staff again to provide increased flexibility and optimize productivity; effectively managed internal resistance to restructuring by selling the merits of the plan; and continued to handle adversity and cultural diversity by diffusing potentially combative situations—the Stuff. As painful as this experience was at the time, it not only contributed to my personal growth, but it caused me to persevere.

"The mark of an exceptional leader is not in the number of hats they must wear, but in the fit of those hats in terms of the leader's ability to communicate, motivate, and establish the level of trust required from those that follow so that a life-changing experience can occur." Unknown

Someone asked the question—
how do you eat an elephant?
Someone responded—one bite at a time.
I say, you don't eat it—it's too big to digest, it's tough,
it's a huge challenge, it's a major undertaking, and it's
awkward. The idea of serving it up would make people
uncomfortable—so why would you!

You're Gonna Step on Something!

I remember a time when you could literally step on someone's toe accidentally and all would be forgiven if you extended an oral courtesy by saying "I'm sorry" or "Excuse me." You could bump into someone while passing on the street and one or both of you would say "Excuse me" and "No problem." You could inadvertently offend someone and detect it based on the person's facial expression, or they might be kind enough to inform you of the offense—"I'm so sorry" or "I meant no harm" was the response. Recall the times when we talked to one another about how their actions or behavior made us feel and the impact it may have had on us physically, mentally, or emotionally. I also recall when we forgave one another for stepping on something, whether it was our actual physical toe, our pride, our ego, or our culture.

How did we as a people and a society find ourselves at a crossroads in which just about everything said or not said, done or not done, implied or interpreted steps on someone else's feelings, heritage, history, beliefs, value systems, or social or organizational culture? In the workplace, when did we transition from oral courtesies of apology for small transgressions to complaints and allegations of a hostile work environment or outcries of discrimination? When did addressing performance-related issues or executing a righteous termination become the mainstay for frivolous agency charges and/or employment lawsuits? When did someone's inability to recover from an unintentionally awkward or clumsy message require them to step down from their position? "Can we talk about it?" has become obsolete, and instead individual or public outcry will call for someone's head on a silver platter, meaning their job, their dignity, or their life's savings. People complain to someone with the expectation that someone will go straighten the person out based on a one-sided version of the issue. We used to be able to just talk about it.

Sometimes we unintentionally create connotations to an ideology of acceptance and appreciation of others and their differences by using terminology that is complicated or too lofty to understand. For example, the term "cultural competence," which refers to one's ability to interact effectively with people of different cultures and socioeconomic backgrounds, implies that there is a point at which one can achieve an acceptable measure of knowledge and agility regarding other people's culture. Culture refers to integrated patterns of human behavior that include the language, thoughts, communications, actions, customs, beliefs, values, and institutions of racial, ethnic, religious, or social groups. Competence implies having the capacity to function effectively as an individual and an organization within the context of the cultural beliefs, behaviors, and needs presented by individuals and their communities (adapted from Cross, 1989).

Cultural competence is comprised of four components: 1) awareness of one's own cultural worldview; 2) attitude toward cultural differences; 3) knowledge of different cultural practices and worldviews; and 4) cross-cultural skills. Developing cultural competence results in an ability to understand, communicate with, and effectively interact with people across cultures. However, people should not bask in the comfort of some false sense of achievement in cultural competence, because it will be at that point that they step on someone's cultural toes and find that the foot in their mouth is attached to their own leg. Cultural competency is a lifelong journey for those who care to and are brave enough to endeavor an exploration of other people's culture. While we never reach the end of this journey to rest in the village of competence or difference, we can sojourn on our way toward greater understanding, an appreciation for mutual respect and civility, and a deeper awareness of social justice issues.

People trip, slip, and on occasion will take a hard fall for something stupid they either said or did or did not say or do. What follows are my own personal missteps; an excellent example of

how well-trained professionals—knowledgeable on issues related to social justice, diversity, and inclusion—can, on occasion,
unintentionally misstep; some messy organizational mishaps and
missteps; and some examples of high-profile political and celebrity missteps that will provide a much broader understanding of
this S*c*uff I keep talking about.

Personal Misstep

My first personal "OMG" story occurred back in 2004 as I was
watching the 2004 Grammy Awards celebration on television. In
a response similar to that of the audience, I felt entertained by
the capstone act performed by OutKast titled "Hey Ya." During
their performance I was smiling and snapping my fingers and
grooving to the beat of what I had always referred to as "that wild
and crazy song." A part of me felt proud of the fact that OutKast
had been in the music industry for a number of years under the
banner of hip-hop, and had finally crossed over into mainstream
America, appealing to audiences outside those we have an affinity to. On this particular evening, OutKast walked away with
a Grammy for the album of the year, in addition to two other
awards. I was genuinely excited about their accomplishments
and felt a real sense of pride.

However, as I was flipping through the *Toledo Blade* newspaper the following morning, the caption in the Peach Plus section
read "OutKast Controversy" and was subtitled "Native Americans
Decry Grammy Performance." As I began to take a closer look
at the costumes and reflected on the actual performance, I was
shocked and appalled at not only what I read in the article, but
at my own behavior the night before. With the realization that I
would be speaking on the topic of diversity in the coming month,
I had to ask myself, how *culturally competent and sensitive* did my
own behavior make me? Was I really that oblivious to the possibility that members from my own affinity group had trampled on

the culture and traditions of another group under the banner of entertainment? While this type of faux pas had historically been reserved for the majority group, the group I have an affinity to (black people) was now being accused of stepping on the culture of Native Americans. The incident gave me pause to ask these questions. Have we in our subcultures become so insensitive that we miss insults to the culture or traditions of other groups than the one we belong to? Have we become immune to the notion that anyone else has the right to be offended?

For the millions of spectators who watched the performance but don't recall the details and for those who were also oblivious of the cultural misstep, what follows is a brief summary of the performance.

Jewish comedian Jack Black introduced the final performance of the Grammy ceremony. A spoken word prelude inferred that Andre 3000 and his companions were coming to save earth in a spaceship that took the form of a Native American tipi. "The natives are getting restless," shouted Jack Black as the authentic native drumming and chanting of a Navajo healing song echoed through the facilities at the Staples Center. But what appeared on the stage were not Native Americans but African-Americans dressed in faux Indian garb. The crowd responded wildly to this spectacle that expressed African-Americans as a racial otherness.

The large curtain rose to reveal a large green tipi. Out of the tipi door burst Andre "3000" Benjamin of the group OutKast with several scantily clad women who danced around the stage in front of the large green tipi. The tipi was/is the symbol of the physical and spiritual home of the Native Americans, not African-Americans. The dancers were sporting face paint, generic green feathers, and fringed costumes as their butts swiveled about the stage among the band members. Antoine "Big Boi" Patton sat at the keyboards wearing a semi-authentic approximation of a Plains Indian war bonnet. Gyrating female dancers integrated eccentric hand and body movements that brought to mind the paintings on ancient Egyptian tombs. What the women's dress brought to mind was something other than feminine native modesty. Andre moved about the stage wearing a fluorescent green skirt with his shirtless upper body exposed, suggesting the attire of native Plains Indian sun dancers.

The USC band, accompanying the performance, walked on stage wearing face paint. The objection to this is that face painting is ceremonial and designates certain rites of passage and recognition among Native Americans. USC's participation/mockery demonstrated their complete ignorance and insensitivity to Native Americans. USC's involvement in this exhibition is particularly troubling given their status as an influential institution with a social and moral obligation to educate future generations (Reum, 2004).

The Native American community was outraged over OutKast's performance for the sheer purpose of commercial entertainment. OutKast's performance stepped on some sacredly held traditions and values that included a "subliminal message of colonial dissent, similar in significance to the Boston Tea party and those colonials who utilized the image and dress of Native American cultural identity, to send a message of 'separateness' from the mother country" (Reum, 2004).

Whatever the intent or purpose of OutKast's performance, Native Americans were way past the "can we talk about it" stage when OutKast refused to apologize or acknowledge any cultural misstep. One thing's for certain and that is OutKast's performance was not a celebration of an authentic Native American tribal relationship. According to Reum (2004), NAJA (Native American Journalists Association) suggests that the comment about the natives being restless should have set off alarms, bells, and whistles among the organizers as well as the media covering the awards show. NAJA further alleged a double standard—in contrast to the Super Bowl incident with Janet Jackson, OutKast's performance was choreographed with the full knowledge of

Grammy organizers. NAJA also questioned how Americans could watch such a travesty for sheer entertainment value and not be offended that even an inkling of "red-face" would be any more acceptable than "blackface minstrelsy" has been to blacks. Perhaps Andre "3000" Benjamin didn't realize he was cheaply imitating regalia, clothing laden with symbolism where everything from the feathers and beads were reserved only for worthy individuals like chiefs. Moreover, many of us were short-sighted in dismissing Native Americans' reaction to the OutKast performance in the same blasé, "I can't see why they're so up-set" language we have justifiably decried when it comes from folks who offend black sensibilities (Reum, 2004). By no means am I attempting to decide what's offensive to someone else. In hindsight, anyone who participated in the performance, who celebrated and/or enjoyed the activity, or who applauded the ef-forts of OutKast was wrong. I was wrong.

A more recent mishap occurred when I was sitting in my office with a staff member discussing a myriad of issues. As our conversation treaded into unchartered territory, I reached for the speaker button to phone a colleague who is also a dear friend. When their voice message kicked on, I left a brief mes-sage asking that they return my call. The conversation between me the staff member had resumed for approximately fifteen minutes when I heard a voice through the speakerphone ask "are you still there"? After being quickly jolted to my senses, I realized what had just occurred and disconnected the call in a panic. You're right, "OMG", the entire conversation was re-corded on my colleague's voice message. Had I not panicked and listened to the automated voice prompts, I would have been able to edit or delete the message. During that fifteen minute open mic conversation, I made some comments in re-sponse to a question about my colleague that was viewed as insensitive. Now, mind you, I could have had this same conver-sation with my colleague with no offense. It was not that I made the comments, but that I was engaging in a conversation with someone else about my colleague that was viewed as hurtful. I must say that I would have been hurt had it happened to me. And yes, someone did come knocking on my door to straighten me out—to fix the messy mishap that I had created by being caught on open mic engaging in a conversation about a colleague. Because my colleague had reached around our relationship for an intervention, I had to take a hands-off approach and could not contact them directly. An inquiry into the incident found no policy violation as this was Scuff, at best. I was informed that my colleague would reach out to me for a conversation I knew would never come. Hence, I suggested that we meet for lunch with the facilitator to talk about how we arrived at such a pivotal crossroad. That much-needed lunch finally occurred where I could face my colleague and dear friend and explain the context of my comments. I was not just asking that my apology be accepted, but was seeking forgiveness from someone that I cared about, and who I hope one day will truly forgive me for the mishap that broke us. While we continue to greet one another and embrace our history together inside the organization, we have yet to move back into the spaces we once shared outside the organization.

You never want to find your
foot in your mouth because it's tough,
it has no flavor, and it's hard to digest.

Social Mishaps/Missteps

About two years ago, a colleague and I attended a national conference solely dedicated to issues of social justice and race relations. My colleague shared a story with me about an incident that occurred during a pre-conference workshop where the presenter stepped on the culture of the majority of the participants. The workshop subject was about facilitating intergroup dialogue and managing "triggers." Triggers in this case were those biases, diversity topics, and stereotype-related sore spots that each of us have buried inside our hearts and minds. The presenter (a white woman) was a well-known diversity champion, experienced train-the-trainer facilitator, and one of the foundational leaders of both premier social justice education and intergroup dialogue organizations in the nation. There were eighty or more participants in the workshop, of which 90 percent or more were people of color, and 75 percent or more of them were black. By mid-morning on the first day, the participants had been pulled into a comfortable space where open, experiential sharing and exchange of ideas came with ease due to the presenter's vast knowledge, facilitation style, and her candidness and openness about her personal experiences. Folks were laughing at her jokes, nodding in agreement when her commentary landed in familiar territory, and participating wholeheartedly during the training exercises.

When the session moderator announced they had come upon the lunch hour and needed to move the participants toward the conference luncheon, that is when it happened. After grabbing the attention of the participants, the presenter said, "I've checked and lunch is scheduled to end at 1:15 this afternoon. We have a lot of ground to cover, so it is important that we begin right at 1:30 p.m. to stay on schedule. In other words, I'm talking 1:30 p.m. my time, not C.P. time." She also emphasized "C.P." by raising her hands and bending both her index and pointer fingers to draw imaginary quotes in the air as she spoke. Tickled by her own humor, she chuckled out loud, turning away from the crowd as she waved for them to exit the room.

The term "C.P. time" or "colored people's time" is a usually correct stereotype that blacks/African-Americans are incapable of punctuality and are chronically tardy in both arriving and beginning events and functions. While she may have been correct in her assumptions to think the group would not arrive back by

1:30 p.m., it was unprofessional and inappropriate for her to say it, particularly because she was presenting on the topic of "triggers." While less offensive than the "N-word," but commonly used within the black community, the term "C.P. time" is reserved for use within the group as an insider-only term. While not all black people agree that the term should be attributed solely to their race, most other people recognize that to do so as a non-black is taboo. However, it would seem that nobody told the presenter, who apparently enjoyed surrounding herself with diverse friends and colleagues on her journey toward cultural competency. Someone along the way shared C.P. time with her but failed to inform her of the rule. The rule being, because of her race she is excluded from using the term, especially in public, during training sessions, and while speaking before a crowd of social justice advocates who are predominantly black.

Had the presenter watched the crowd's reaction as they left the room or laughed a little softer, then perhaps she would have detected the shock on people's faces or heard the breathy gasps in the air. In an instant, the presenter fell off the cliff of the cultural competency mountain and into the valley of politically incorrect ignorance, and she had no clue! In a delayed response to her comment, several black women mumbled, "No she didn't." My colleague says that she personally hung onto the hope that this had all been a setup for the afternoon session to further demonstrate and explore how to handle oneself after being "triggered." At the time, she had no idea how wrong she was. However, rest assured, this group addressed the issue with the presenter directly after lunch and spent a considerable amount of time doing so.

Prior to the session starting, a few black folks took the opportunity to train-the-trainer and educate the presenter on boundaries. By the time all the participants had returned to their seats, the presenter had received a PhD in "don't ever do that again!" Humbly and red-faced she greeted the group and began to slow-walk her foot out of her mouth with an apology and self-loathing. As you can see, hypocrisy does not aid digestion as the participants returned from lunch with heartburn toward the presenter. While it only took about five minutes for the presenter to regain the confidence of the group, I can imagine it seemed much longer to her, which she accomplished by admitting that she was just as apt to fall into the occasional insensitive behavior trap as anybody else and asked for forgiveness.

I never considered my professional development as a journey until I enrolled in a master's program. The program was one of the best learning experiences I have had in my life. The program format was a cohort of thirty-seven students who attended class together, one weekend a month, over a twenty-one-month period. The breakdown of the group consisted of thirty-three women and four men; nine African-Americans, one Native American, and twenty-seven white students. Cultural differences were definitely a factor as they related to the group's dynamics.

As cohort members settled into a monthly routine, relationships were born and friendships were formed. Cultural clashes emerged as people began the process of self-expression on sensitive issues such as sexual orientation, religion, politics, race, and the like. The biggest of these clashes occurred when a young black woman asked the class to stand up and join hands while she led the group in prayer for two of our cohort members who had lost a student to suicide that same weekend. Some cohort members felt forced to participate even though they did not want to. As we began to debrief the incident, it became evident that culture was at the root of the dissention among the group—sometimes black people do not realize that prayer or praising God in public can be viewed as insensitive by making assumptions about other people's faith. In a "Christian country" it is easy to step on someone else's religious beliefs or desire not to have any. It's like black people who think that nobody knows or loves Jesus the way they do. Well, black people are not the most religious group of people in Western society; they're just more emotional about it than some other groups.

This experience was a pivotal turning point for the cohort, strengthening the group's ability to effectively communicate with one another and to professionally agree to disagree. While some of us were unable to overcome those hurdles, others of us will remain lifelong friends.

Organizational Mishaps/Missteps

I recall a senior level administrator who reached out to me for assistance in facilitating an issue when they managed to step on someone's cultural toe three days into their new job. In this situation, the cultural breach was of organizational protocol. This leader did not follow the traditional steps regarding a particular process because they were too new to the organization and knew only how things were done in their previous organization. While there were no real rules in writing, in practice, most employees understood the way things ought to be done. The administrator's mistake was viewed by one person as so egregious that they threatened to resign from the project team if the breach was not corrected.

I also recall a male employee asking for a consultation about how to handle what he perceived to be an inappropriate communication on the part of his supervisor. While the organization has an LGBT (lesbian, gay, bisexual, and transgender) affinity group, not every person who has an affinity to the group is openly LGBT. This employee's concern was that his supervisor had identified him as a contact person for the LGBT affinity group in a group email to people not in that group. As a relatively new employee, he had not disclosed his sexual orientation to anyone in the office and was offended that his supervisor would make assumptions about his sexual orientation, his membership in a specific affinity group, and (if he were gay) if he wanted that information to be publicly shared. While many of us have made assumptions about others based on many different characteristics, did the supervisor deserve to lose their job for the assumptions they made about their employee? Absolutely not! As it turned out, the supervisor sent the email in an attempt to appear as an advocate, unintentionally making some assumptions based on their observations. While the employee never confirmed the assumptions made by the supervisor, what occurred was not discrimination based on his assumed sexual orientation, but on a lack of communication between him and his supervisor. More importantly, the real issue of concern was not discrimination, but the supervisor's misguided attempts to direct internal resources to the LGBT affinity group.

Political and/or Celebrity Missteps

When I use the term "misstep," what I am not referring to is events such as the egregious incident with Don Imus, who referred to Rutgers women's basketball players as "nappy-headed hoes." The comment was intentional, outrageous, inappropriate, and a micro-assault (a conscious and intentional action or slur, such as using racial epithets) at best. Imus' firing was righteous and justified. Unfortunately, this termination only occurred on the heels of the public's outcry for his termination alongside major corporate sponsors' withdrawal of advertisement dollars from the network.

Nor am I referring to the comments like those made by Republican Majority Leader Senator Trent Lott, who in 2002 lost his leadership position after using racially charged language. According to Elliott (2010) the Mississippi lawmaker said that "if then-Sen. Strom Thurmond's 1948 pro-segregation presidential bid had been successful, the country would have been better off." Senator Lott's comments were intended to set the gains made by African-Americans back to the Jim Crow era, a time in which state and local laws mandated segregation in all public facilities (public schools, public transportation, restrooms, restaurants, drinking fountains, and even the U.S. Military), with supposedly "separate but equal" status for blacks. However, in reality, the treatment and accommodations afforded to blacks were far inferior to those provided to whites.

I would be remiss not to mention Indiana GOP U.S. Senate candidate Richard Murdock, who ignited a media storm over comments he made related to a question on the issue of abortion. During a debate, Murdock said, "Life is that gift from God. I think that even when life begins in that horrible situation of rape, it is something God intended to happen." Murdock lost the election and is still probably chewing on that tasty piece of foot he couldn't get out of his mouth. Along the same lines was the ridiculous comment made by Missouri GOP Senate candidate Rep. Todd Akin, who infamously asserted that women don't get pregnant from "legitimate rape." While both missteps were career-derailing faux pas of 2012, they were also absolutely stupid and insensitive comments from prospective political leaders. Sometimes in politics, when you make a mistake or misstep, you lose the right to play.

However, not all situations are so clear. A more complicated one involved then Fox Senior News Analyst and NPR Commentator Juan Williams, who made the comment on Fox News that "when I get on a plane, I got to tell you, if I see people who are in Muslim garb, and I think, you know, they're identifying themselves first and foremost as Muslims, I get worried. I get nervous." This comment was made in the context of a discussion about terrorism which took place on *The O'Reilly Factor*, part of the FOX network. In response NPR's chief executive, Vivian Schiller, issued a written statement saying, in part, that "Williams' remarks on *The O'Reilly Factor* were inconsistent with our editorial standards and practices and undermined his credibility as a news analyst with NPR." When NPR fired Mr. Williams for his remarks, public outcry contended that the termination was overkill, but NPR had already taken the option of talking off the table. Not only was it overkill, it silenced an opportunity for open dialogue about cultural perceptions and misunderstandings that breed intolerance. When Schiller reached for the rule book, she ended a process of cultural misunderstandings which resulted in a major misstep for Mr. Williams.

Another case in which a misstep was blown out of proportion involved Shirley Sherrod, a director of the Department of Agriculture of rural development in Georgia. Ms. Sherrod was forced to resign in July 2010 after a conservative blogger misrepresented her in a video clip that appeared to show her admitting racial antipathy toward a white farmer. Mr. Vilsack conceded that he had ordered Ms. Sherrod's firing in haste without knowing that the video clip from a speech she gave to the NAACP had been taken out of context. Vilsack said that he had acted on his own, and that there was "no pressure from the White House." While public outcry had demanded and was given Ms. Sherrod's head on a silver platter (her job), by the end of the day she had gained instant fame and emerged as the heroine of a compelling story about race and redemption.

And last but not least, let us recall the political misstep by Senate Democratic Leader Harry Reid, who apologized for saying then-candidate Obama's race would help rather than hurt his run for the presidency. Senator Reid was impressed with Obama's oratorical talents and believed that America was ready to embrace a black presidential candidate. Senator Reid described Barack Obama as a "light-skinned" African-American "with no Negro dialect, unless he wanted to have one." Reid's comments were made in 2010 and revealed in a 2008 book by *Time* magazine's Mark Halperin and *New York Magazine's* John Heilemann titled "Game Change." When the excerpt/comments hit the Internet, Reid released a statement expressing regret for the poor choice of words and apologized for offending any and all Americans, especially African-Americans, for the improper comments.

Now would it ruin me politically to say that I agree with Reid's private assessment of Obama's skin color and dialect? Let's hope not. If I were a betting person, I would say that a large majority of the American population, African-Americans in particular, would agree that the comments, although politically incorrect, were on point. Reid's comments were an unsuccessful attempt to articulate that Americans were ready to embrace a smart, educated black man who's earned his stripes in the political arena, a man who knew how to present himself and was the total package. I believe that's what he meant! Just because he said it badly does not make it incorrect—maybe politically.

Let's face it, words matter. But let's stop getting caught up on every word people use and try to hear what's really being said. Sometimes people's attempt at code-switching ends up being a botched job of trying to articulate what they really mean. According to Biber (1995) the term "code-switching," as used in this context, does not refer to the practice of moving back and forth between two languages, but rather to switching among registers as is practiced by speakers of African-American Vernacular English as they move from less formal to more formal settings. Registers are used to indicate the degree of formality in language use that is determined by factors such as social occasion, purpose, and audience.

How we show up to other people is based on what we think they need from us in a given situation.
We are many things to many different people.
Most of us code-switch depending on the audience—business, professional, family, friends, community, etc.

There is no question that Senator Reid's comment about "light-skinned" and "Negro dialect" reflected a poor choice of words, but the mere use of the words should not distract the American public from its continued focus on securing health care or creating jobs for its people. Taking the lead from now President Obama, we sometimes have to allow people to make mistakes with us and keep it moving—it's just S*c*uff. Did the world end? No. Did the comments ruin Obama's chances at the presidency? Absolutely not! Did the comments keep Obama up all night and hurt his feelings? Most probably not!

Likewise, all words and comments should not distract in the workplace as colleagues attempt to build relationships and community across organizations, departments, campuses, and the like. Sometimes people are going to fumble the ball, trip on their words, or slur their phrase because they don't know everything they need to know about every subculture to keep them out of trouble. When everything in your cultural bag reflects your own life, cultural clashes are hard to avoid. This lack of understanding and a failure to communicate can get translated into S*c*uff. Sometimes we make this S*c*uff bigger than it needs to be. Instead of blowing off the dust, some people find the need to add water and stir because they like it messy—they like playing in the mud.

Sometimes we just don't know what we don't know!

People no longer talk through the messy mishaps, misunderstandings, missteps, or miscommunications in the workplace or broader society. Instead, they hide behind electronic devices and/or social media to express themselves. Or, they complain to a third party and expect results. We as a people will never really get to know one another if we aren't allowed to make some mistakes or missteps with one another while journeying through this diverse world. It is better to forgive one another for mistakes and/or missteps and to begin an open and candid dialogue in order to create a shared understanding of one another's cultures.

Of all the differences we have with each other, race is one of the messiest. As a broader society, we tiptoe around the subject of race as if it doesn't exist knowing full well that it impacts people of color on a daily basis and plays a major role in people's everyday psyches. I'm still troubled by the notion that people can say they don't see color when they look at people. How can this be? How about this? How about as long as a comment related to race is not intentionally insensitive, offensive, flagrantly racist (such as the "N" word), why can we not make reference to race in the context of the society we live in? It is my observation that black people, in particular, will openly and publicly talk about race, though most other races and/or ethnic groups appear uncomfortable openly engaging in public conversations on the subject. But, when white people do it or make a stray remark or comment, they're labeled as being insensitive or politically incorrect, and the expectation is that somebody's head or "behind" should be front and center on a silver platter. Hence, some of the reasons other groups stay away from the subject.

Let's take our lead from President Obama and forgive people for making mistakes with us and move on. President Obama quickly accepted Reid's apology by saying "as far as I am concerned, the book is closed." Obama has since accepted apologies about additional past comments that might be considered racially insensitive including when Joe Biden called Obama "the first mainstream African-American who is articulate and bright and clean and a nice-looking guy." Though these remarks could have been taken to mean that it is unusual for a black person to be intelligent and well-spoken, Obama, in the complimentary spirit they were intended, moved past them, and invited Biden to be his running mate.

Playing the Cards

People will "play a card" if they believe that it will give them the upper hand or some advantage in a situation—or better yet, they use it as leverage in an attempt to get the outcome they're looking for. For example, I was recently watching a rerun from the popular *Two and a Half Men*. In this sitcom, Charlie and Alan are brothers, and Alan has lived with Charlie rent-free for the entire series. During this episode, Alan accepted an invitation from Teddy (their mother's new boyfriend and soon-to-be fiancé) to go to Las Vegas for a weekend. Charlie, on the other hand, saw the invitation as underhanded and initially refused to go. So, when Alan informed Charlie that he immediately accepted the invitation, Charlie said to Alan, "You're going to be homeless," meaning if Alan were to go to Las Vegas with Teddy, Charlie would put Alan out of his house. Alan responded, "Why do you always have to play that card?" It's the "this is my house and I can put you out if I don't like what you do or say" card. Charlie's comment was an overt attempt to hold Alan's decision-making hostage (going to Vegas) with the threat of an unpleasant action (being put out on the street) if Alan didn't see things his way (tell Teddy he would not go on the trip to Vegas). Charlie leveraged a threat to get the outcome he wanted. Employees sometimes do the same thing.

Inside as well as outside of organizations people have a tendency to shuffle the deck and play one of the many cards from the hand they have been dealt (race, color, creed, age, sex, sexual orientation, religion, national origin, ability, veteran status, socioeconomic status, etc.). In most organizations, what gets leveraged up through the internal complaint process are allegations of harassment and/or discrimination based on some protected characteristic, when in most situations, what is at the core of the issue is S*cuff* (**S**omething *T*hat **U** **F**ind **F**rustrating*"*) most likely grounded in a cultural misstep or a failure to communicate. Each and every one of us has at least one "card" to play that can be attributed to one or more of the protected characteristics enforceable by either the EEOC or the OCR statute.

African-Americans have been accused of overplaying the race card. However, when people feel backed into a corner or are at that boiling point in which they have shopped their issues within the department without resolution, they will play that trump card—their ace in the hole—the card that gains them the most leverage in order to have their issue addressed formally in pursuit of satisfaction or to have the behavior(s) in question stopped.

I recall sitting in a concurrent break-out session on "micro-inequities" at a conference in Lima, Ohio, at Rhodes State College. A colleague commented to the presenter that he gets so angry when people say that black people always overplay the race card when expressing or articulating the most subtle micro-inequities. I chimed in to say that when people say that to me, I say, "Most people have some type of card they can play—there is the age card, the disabilities card, the LGBT card, the religious card, the national origin card, and the list goes on." And while black people may reach for the race card more often than some of their other cards, it is because race has historically been grounded in issues black people face with the majority culture. However, I recognize that not everything that happens to black people is necessarily grounded in race. Sometimes, we as black people need to check ourselves, take ownership for some of our own foolishness and Scuff. If your boss is taking you on for your performance, you may need to assess your performance and ask yourself if you're doing what you're supposed to be doing. If your boss is taking you on for your attendance, you might need to show up more than three days a week or not be routinely late.

Right on the heels of this publication of Scuff I was asked by a colleague for some airtime and we agreed on an after-hours meeting off the premises. This woman was having some issues in her organization and wanted an objective perspective, an ear or a sounding board as she would later call it. She spent more than three hours talking about how her manager had totally dismantled her unit since his hire by moving her second-in-command out of her unit to a direct reporting line under him, which in her opinion put their roles at odds. She talked about how her manager had also reduced her frontline resources, making her ineffective, and had begun scheduling routine meetings with her staff without her. The final straw was an email exchange that she sent to someone she thought she could trust that ended up squarely planted in the in-box of her boss' boss. Yes, my thoughts exactly! The "grand finale" came the day she called me for airtime. Her boss had just presented her with what she referred to as a performance evaluation but what read more like a PIP—a Performance Improvement Plan. Now mind you, she wasn't looking for me to co-sign on her perceptions; as she adamantly stated several times during the conversation, she was prepared to own some of her S*uff. She had just never found herself in a situation like this before professionally and didn't know what to do or how to handle it. Some of the S*uff she acknowledged as change that occurs when a new leader steps to the helm and assembles their own team. It was probably around her third iteration of personal as well as professional ownership that I finally said to her, "I have to tell you this; if you were a black woman sitting here telling this story, I promise you you'd be wrapping all this S*uff around your race. You'd be telling me that this is only happening to you because you're black," to which we both roared with laughter. While this was one of those well-intended white women who actually "gets it" and could find humor in my comments from a diversity perspective, many other white people are playing other cards at an all-time high. What follows are some examples of card-carrying white people.

A white man alleged discrimination based on a disability during the admissions interview process. Actually, no one on the review board was aware that the applicant had previously been diagnosed with bipolar disorder. He was not on record as having a disability, no one in the school treated him as a person with a disability, and he never asked for an accommodation for any disabling condition. While the GPA was a component of the overall admissions and evaluation process, the interview was where professional standards were assessed and was most important in the application process. What the student alleged as discrimination based on a disability was actually the board's response to a poor showing during the interview process. In spite of the student's considerable academic achievements, he was deemed unacceptable based solely on his responses and overall behavior during the interview. It was determined that the student would have great difficulty relating to patients and colleagues; consequently, he was denied admission which had nothing to do with a disability.

In another case, a white woman alleged retaliation for filing a previous complaint and sex discrimination as the reason she was denied promotion. In higher education, faculty are evaluated in three areas—teaching, research, and service. While there was evidence of a heavier teaching load, performance challenges in two of the three areas were less than satisfactory. Unfortunately, her unsuccessful attempts at promotion were not because of her gender, but rather her inability to achieve success in all three areas. Moreover, what she viewed as retaliation for filing a previous complaint was basically an ongoing discussion with her supervisor about her performance. Because she remained unsatisfied with the outcome of her Scuff, she continued to shop her issues out to external organizations in pursuit of a different outcome.

A white man who attended a national recruiting event alleged discrimination based on his age. While the applicant appeared to have a respectable career in his discipline, he was definitely not someone the recruitment committee would have even considered interviewing because of two factors having nothing to do with his age. First, he had never published anything, let alone anything of a scholarly nature. Second, his expertise and teaching/research interests were in areas that were not an area for which the school was recruiting. The recruitment committee automatically declined to interview anyone with primary teaching interests in areas other than those the school had identified as critical needs. So the applicant's combination of not having expertise or interest in an area for which the school was hiring and his total lack of any record of scholarship made him someone in which the school had no interest. This particular applicant, like hundreds of others, was culled from the pile very quickly for legitimate reasons having nothing to do with his age. Again, people will shop their issues because they believe they have nothing to lose by doing so and see no other options before them.

A faculty member alleged discrimination based on his national origin after the school failed to renew his contract. The instructor had received unsatisfactory feedback in his teaching evaluations that indicated he never came to class prepared and that he didn't follow the protocol of the school's tenor. The instructor acknowledged that he had previously been informed that his application was less competitive, he was considered unorganized, often came to class unprepared, and based on his professional references, he failed to teach the concepts as outlined in the departmental syllabus and course description. He insisted that students did not like him because he usually taught what he felt students should learn, and he set higher standards than what was expected. While some student evaluations reflected that he communicated poorly, he insisted the comments were biased toward his nationality and accent. Fortunately, the department chair, who also has a heavy accent, attempted to explain that it is not uncommon that students make comments about faculty in professional schools who have accents being more difficult to understand. The chair also shared that due to his own accent he sometimes receives such comments from students and pointed out that such situations challenge both faculty and students to work harder toward effective communication. This faculty member's national origin or accent had nothing to do with the reasons his contract was not renewed. It simply was not renewed because of subpar performance and weak references.

While none of these scenarios were grounded in illegal harassment or discrimination protected by legislation, they do reflect common examples of the S*cuff* I keep talking about. When people are at their boiling point or when they feel backed into a corner, most will reach for a card to play as they have nothing to lose by doing so. In each of the scenarios, the complainant was frustrated by a series of events that ultimately culminated in their filing a formal discrimination complaint with the external agency that has jurisdiction over such issues. With respect to any aspect of the employment process (search and screening, recruiting, hiring, compensation, professional development, promotions, transfers and terminations), employees will raise a myriad of issues when those employment decisions adversely impact their ability to be successful or remain gainfully employed. Employees have a right to complain and have nothing to lose by doing so, only something to potentially gain. So when employees don't get the outcome they seek internally, they clearly have nothing to lose by playing their trump card with one of the federal agencies.

According to the Equal Employment Opportunity Commission (EEOC) statistics as shown in **Table I**, roughly 100,000 charges were filed each year from 1997 to 2011. Race continues to be the area with the largest percentage of charges around 36 percent; sex discrimination charges are in second place with 29 percent; and age and disabilities follow in a close third with about 24 percent each. Over a four-year average,

- Of the race-based charges depicted in **Table II**, 9 percent were settled, 14 percent were administratively closed, 68 percent received a "no reasonable cause" finding, and only 4 percent were found to have "reasonable cause."
- Eleven percent of the sex-based charges depicted in **Table III** were settled, 19 percent were administratively closed, 59 percent received a "no reasonable cause" finding, and only 5 percent were found to have "reasonable cause."
- Age Discrimination in Employment Act charges depicted in **Table IV** show that 9 percent were settled, 21 percent were administratively closed, 62 percent received a

"no reasonable cause" finding, and only 3 percent were found to have "reasonable cause."

- For Americans with Disabilities Act of 1990 charges depicted in **Table V**, only 11 percent were settled, 17 percent were administratively closed, 61 percent received a "no reasonable cause" finding, and only 5 percent were found to have "reasonable cause."
- All four categories averaged only 1.27 percent successful conciliation agreements.

While most charge categories have slowly trended upward over the past fifteen years according to EEOC's statistics, age-discrimination charges have hit an all-time high, up by almost 30 percent from 16,548 claims filed in 2006 to 23,465 claims filed in 2011. Such an increase can be attributed to an increasing number of aging employees in the workforce, particularly the baby-boomer generation, who watched their retirement savings plummet alongside the stock and housing markets. In addition, laid-off and unemployed older workers may be taking more legal action to recover their jobs or lost wages because it's taking them longer than younger workers to find new employment. Older workers also struggle against perceptions about their lack of stamina, physical and mental abilities using technology, as well as their inability to adapt to change.

When the EEOC was asked if investigations show that charges of discrimination are more likely an indication of an illegal act of discrimination versus poor communication between employee and manager, poor management, or a disgruntled employee, they responded that in looking at the aggregate, most claims are not frivolous. The EEOC also suggest that often people are blown off by management and they have nowhere else to go.

Table I
U.S. Equal Employment Opportunity Commission
Charge Statistics
FY 2008 Through FY 2011

The number for total charges reflects the number of individual charge filings. Because individuals often file charges claiming multiple types of discrimination, the number of total charges for any given fiscal year will be less than the total number of the ten types of discrimination.

	FY 2008	FY 2009	FY 2010	FY 2011
Total Charges	95,402	93,277	99,922	99,947
Race	33,937	33,579	35,890	35,395
	35.6%	36.0%	35.9%	35.4%
Sex	28,372	28,028	29,029	28,534
	29.7%	30.0%	29.1%	28.5%
National Origin	10,601	11,134	11,304	11,833
	11.1%	11.9%	11.3%	11.8%
Religion	3,273	3,386	3,790	4,151
	3.4%	3.6%	3.8%	4.2%
Color	2,698	2,943	2,780	2,832
	2.8%	3.2%	2.8%	2.8%
Retaliation - All Statutes	32,690	33,613	36,258	37,334
	34.3%	36.0%	36.3%	37.4%
Retaliation - Title VII only	28,698	28,948	30,948	31,429
	30.1%	31.0%	31.0%	31.4%
Age	24,582	22,778	23,264	23,465
	25.8%	24.4%	23.3%	23.5%
Disability	19,453	21,451	25,165	25,742
	20.4%	23.0%	25.2%	25.8%
Equal Pay Act	954	942	1,044	919
	1.0%	1.0%	1.0%	0.9%
Genetic Information Nondiscrimination Act (GINA)			201	245
			0.2%	0.2%

http://www.eeoc.gov/eeoc/statistics/enforcement/charges.cfm

Table II - Race-Based EEOC Charges

The following chart represents the total number of charge receipts filed and resolved under Title VII alleging race-based discrimination.

	FY 2008	FY 2009	FY 2010	FY 2011
Receipts	33,937	33,579	35,890	35,395
Resolutions	28,321	31,129	37,559	40,534
Resolutions By Type				
Settlements	3,069	3,065	3,325	3,307
	10.8%	9.8%	8.9%	8.2%
Administrative Closures	3,964	4,803	5,018	5,719
	14.0%	15.4%	13.4%	14.1%
No Reasonable Cause	18,792	20,530	26,319	28,602
	66.4%	66.0%	70.1%	70.6%
Reasonable Cause	1,061	1,201	1,330	1,248
	3.7%	3.9%	3.5%	3.1%
Successful Conciliations	355	392	377	322
	1.3%	1.3%	1.0%	0.8%
Unsuccessful Conciliations	706	809	953	926
	2.5%	2.6%	2.5%	2.3%

Table III - Sex-Based EEOC Charges

The following chart represents the total number of charge receipts filed and resolved under Title VII alleging sex-based discrimination.

	FY 2008	FY 2009	FY 2010	FY 2011
Receipts	28,372	28,028	29,029	28,534
Resolutions	24,018	26,618	30,914	32,789
Resolutions By Type				
Settlements	2,842	2,748	3,138	3,200
	11.8%	10.3%	10.2%	9.8%
Administrative Closures	4,563	5,701	5,727	5,728
	19.0%	21.4%	18.5%	17.5%
No Reasonable Cause	13,670	15,139	18,709	20,660
	56.9%	56.9%	60.5%	63.0%
Reasonable Cause	1,297	1,329	1,566	1,421
	5.4%	5.0%	5.1%	4.3%
Successful Conciliations	382	407	475	510
	1.6%	1.5%	1.5%	1.6%
Unsuccessful Conciliations	915	922	1,091	911
	3.8%	3.5%	3.5%	2.8%

Table IV - Age-Based EEOC Charges

The following chart represents the total number of charge receipts filed and resolved under the Age Discrimination in Employment Act (ADEA).

	FY 2008	FY 2009	FY 2010	FY 2011
Receipts	24,582	22,778	23,264	23,465
Resolutions	21,415	20,529	24,800	26,080
Resolutions By Type				
Settlements	1,974	1,935	2,250	2,231
	9.2%	9.4%	9.1%	8.6%
Administrative Closures	6,387	4,031	4,167	4,230
	29.8%	19.6%	16.8%	16.2%
No Reasonable Cause	11,124	12,788	16,308	17,454
	51.9%	62.3%	65.8%	66.9%
Reasonable Cause	678	614	753	796
	3.2%	3.0%	3.0%	3.1%
Successful Conciliations	220	202	252	273
	1.0%	1.0%	1.0%	1.0%
Unsuccessful Conciliations	458	412	501	523
	2.1%	2.0%	2.0%	2.0%

Table V - Disability-Based EEOC Charges

The following charts represent the total number of charge receipts filed and resolved under the Americans with Disabilities Act (ADA).

	FY 2008	FY 2009	FY 2010	FY 2011
Receipts	19,453	21,451	25,165	25,742
Resolutions	16,705	18,776	24,401	27,873
Resolutions By Type				
Settlements	2,079	2,065	2,597	2,843
	12.4%	11.0%	10.6%	10.2%
Administrative Closures	2,889	3,358	3,980	4,315
	17.3%	17.9%	16.3%	15.5%
No Reasonable Cause	9,760	11,174	15,182	17,727
	58.4%	59.5%	62.2%	63.6%
Reasonable Cause	919	962	1,186	1,272
	5.5%	5.1%	4.9%	4.6%
Successful Conciliation	362	408	439	491
	2.2%	2.2%	1.8%	1.8%
Unsuccessful Conciliation	557	554	747	781
	3.3%	3.0%	3.1%	2.8%

There is a distinction between discrimination and a legitimate business decision. Employers of choice want to retain their best employees regardless of age, gender, race, or any other characteristic currently protected by law. I contend that while the claims may not be frivolous, according to the agency's statistics the majority are also not illegal harassment or illegal discrimination. Previous **Tables II–V** indicate that 83 percent of the race-based charges were either administratively closed or the agency found no reasonable cause. Meaning, the EEOC found no reasonable cause to believe that discrimination occurred based upon the evidence obtained during the investigation. Similar results were found for sex-based charges 78 percent, 82 percent for age-based charges, and 78 percent for disability-based charges. Moreover, all four categories settled less than 12 percent on average of their charges and only 1.27 percent on average ended with a successful conciliation agreement.

Again, when people have reached their boiling point and feel backed into a corner, most will reach for a card to play as they have nothing to lose by doing so—frivolous or not. Moreover, the poor economy and the meteoric rise in layoffs also contribute to the rise in charges. Regardless of the economies of scale, most employees will raise a myriad of employment-related issues when decisions adversely impact their livelihood as they have nothing to lose by doing so, only something to gain. As has been my experience, some organizations will engage in settlement talks in order to ascertain whether an issue can be resolved for some nuisance value just to get it off their plate. Therefore, when employees don't get the outcome they seek internally, they clearly have nothing to lose by playing their trump card with one of the federal agencies.

While the EEOC's statistics are not disaggregated by race or ethnicity, what follows is an analysis of an organization's complaint data over a four-year period by race to ascertain if black people overplay the race card as suggested by some. According to **Table VI,** black people raised race-based complaints at a much higher rate than other groups. While black people are only about 10 percent of the total workforce in this organization **(Table VII),** they raise issues of race on average of 73.2 percent of the total race-based complaints **(Table VI).** And although black people raise more issues on race, black women, in particular, raise more issues of race on average of 47.3 percent **(Table VIII)** of the total race-based complaints than black males or other groups combined.

In addition, **Table IX** is a snapshot of complaint data by approach over a four-year period which indicates that on average 79 percent of the issues raised were addressed using an internal hybrid of empowerment, consultation, and/or facilitated conversations—viewed as S*c*u*ff, whereas about 10 percent on average were formally investigated.

Table VI

2009 – 2012
Race-Based Discrimination Complaints
by Race

	2009	2010	2011	2012
Asian	3	0	1	0
	12.5%	3.2%	4.0%	0.0%
Black/African American	17	20	18	13
	70.8%	64.5%	72.0%	85.7%
Hispanic/Latino	0	1	3	1
	0.0%	3.2%	12.0%	7.1%
Native American	0	0	0	0
	0.0%	0.0%	0.0%	0.0%
Unknown	0	1	1	0
	0.0%	3.2%	4.0%	0.0%
White	4	8	2	1
	16.7%	25.8%	8.0%	7.1%
Total	24	30	25	15

Note: Unknown = race indicators not known due to anonymous reporting

Table VII

2012 Organizational Workforce Data

By EEO Category

Job Group	Total	Black	Hisp	Asian	NatAm	NHOPI	Two+	Min	White	Fem	Male
Faculty (All ranks)	4395	192	99	728	8	6	57	1090	3305	1946	2449
Executives	128	11	2	7	0	0	3	23	105	50	78
Professional	2247	187	21	116	3	0	32	359	1888	1531	716
Clerical	1053	210	12	17	4	0	9	252	801	973	80
Technical	653	82	14	70	3	0	9	178	475	422	231
Skilled Craft	141	16	1	1	0	0	4	22	119	7	134
Service Maintenance	287	168	11	4	1	0	4	188	99	122	165
Total	8904	866	160	943	19	6	118	2112	6792	5051	3853
% of Workforce		9.7%	1.8%	10.6%	0.2%	0.1%	1.3%	23.7%	76.3%	56.7%	43.3%

Table VIII

2009—2012
Race-Based Discrimination Complaints
by Gender

| | 2009 | | 2010 | | 2011 | | 2012 | |
	Female	Male	Female	Male	Female	Male	Female	Male
Asian	0	3	0	0	1	0	0	0
	0.0%	12.5%	0.0%	0.0%	4.2%	0.0%	0.0%	0.0%
Black/African-American	11	6	14	6	12	6	7	6
	45.8%	25.0%	46.7%	20.0%	50.0%	25.0%	46.7%	40.0%
Hispanic/Latino	0	0	1	0	2	1	1	0
	0.0%	0.0%	3.3%	0.0%	8.3%	4.2%	6.7%	0.0%
Native American	0	0	0	0	0	0	0	0
	0.0%	0.0%	0.0%	0.0%	0.0%	0.0%	0.0%	0.0%
White	0	4	4	4	1	1	1	0
	0.0%	16.7%	13.3%	13.3%	4.2%	4.2%	6.7%	0.0%
Total	11	13	19	10	16	8	9	6
	24		29		24		15	

Note: One unknown gender indicator in 2010 and 2011 not reflected in summary totals

Table IX

2009 – 2012
Complaint Data by Approach

Approach	2009	2010	2011	2012
Consultation	93	120	138	129
	79.5%	80.0%	75.8%	80.6%
Mediation	2	3	1	3
	1.7%	2.0%	0.6%	1.9%
Investigation	10	7	29*	16
	8.6%	4.7%	15.9%	10.0%
Agency Charges	12	18	14	10
	10.3%	12.0%	7.7%	6.3%
Court/Lawsuits	0	2	0	2
	0.0%	1.3%	0.0%	1.3%
Total Complaints	**117**	**150**	**182**	**160**

* Of the 29 investigations, 19 were Salary Equity Reviews of which 17 were female

How Did We Get Here?

What people bring with them into the workplace is who they are—their culture, attitudes, beliefs, value systems, customs, traditions, as well as their baggage and opinions on every subject known to man. The workplace has even become a place in which some colleagues are afraid of approaching someone of interest because if they are rejected, the receiving party may feel inclined to raise issues of sexual harassment. If both parties in a specific scenario are on equal footing (no reporting relationship where one is in a position of power over the other), in such a case the incident is no more than a rejected pass—no harm, no foul.

I recall an incident where a woman who hailed from the western region of the country frequently used what she referred to as "terms of endearment"—"hon," "dear," "babe," and "sweetie"—when referring to some of her colleagues. One of her male colleagues misinterpreted those terms as expressing an amorous interest in him and he began to pursue her. While her intentions may have been very different, her actions appeared reciprocal. Specifically, she engaged in what could be perceived as flirtatious conversations, accepted a date, specifically, an invitation to dinner and a movie, and continued to seek out his friendship in the workplace. She raised issues of sexual harassment when her boyfriend confronted her after her male colleague began calling her at home. However, instead of informing her colleague that she was no longer receptive to his advances, had no real interest in dating him, or had changed her mind, she raised her concerns internally to get him off her back since they both worked in the same organization. In essence, she wanted someone else to clean up the mess she'd made and go straighten this guy out.

In my current role at a relatively large institution, I am responsible for monitoring compliance with the organization's anti-harassment and anti-discrimination policies and federal and state equal opportunity and nondiscrimination laws and regulations. This includes investigating and resolving discrimination and harassment complaints to determine if compliance or policy violations exist, to circumvent potential litigation, and to propose and/or implement corrective action(s) and interventions. As you can imagine, I have just about seen and heard it all.

But let's face it, colleagues are going to approach one another in an attempt to establish a relationship with someone they may be attracted to or interested in. When approximately 40,000 different constituents come into an organization on a daily basis, some of those people will find themselves attracted to one another and, consequently, they will date. It is unrealistic to think that you can put 40,000 or more people in a space five days a week, eight hours a day, without some chemistry or sparks flying. However, people are entitled to an official rejection that says "I'm not interested, stop asking," or "stop bothering me" before alleging sexual harassment. I assert that the only way someone will know whether or not you are interested in them is if they approach you and ask you out. The mere act of a peer asking another peer out is not harassment just because the invitation was extended in the classroom or in the workplace. If one party is not interested, my advice would be to use the same type of response or approach you would if the invitation had been extended in a social setting (a wedding, a club, birthday party, etc.). If someone smiles or giggles their way through a conversation with a pursuing party, the behavior may be mistaken as a sign of interest—that you're "playing hard to get" and are likewise interested, or that you might enjoy being pursued though you may not want to actually date. The pursuing party will not know that you're not interested unless you **actually tell** them you are not.

If employees or students complain to an official office in the organization because someone asked them out, the pursuing party often perceives the act as a cowardly approach to getting other people to do your dirty work. How hard is it to tell someone you have no romantic interest in them? The pursuing party is entitled to clear rejection—you owe them that. However, if they continue to pursue you after you have told them you are not interested, this can create an issue of harassment. Being pursued in the workplace isn't inherently illegal or inappropriate behavior, though it can be risky, particularly if the person doing the pursuing is in a position of power over you (such as a supervisor over an employee or faculty member over a student).

In our personal relationships we accept and/or tolerate infractions, disappointments, hurt, pain, heartaches, dishonesty—violations of trust, infidelities, miscommunications, disrespect, and a long list of other transgressions that frustrate and infuriate us. More specifically, with a spouse, significant other, or partner, we forgive transgressions when they don't call, show up late, stand us up, or maybe forget our birthday or anniversary. Somehow we manage to talk through the issues, work it out, and navigate our way through these transgressions, which is part of the relationship-building process. We discuss, apologize, forgive, and most often are able to move forward. While there may be an initial premature departure of ways, one party may eventually muster up the courage to be the bigger person who initiates a dialogue to talk through the issues that created the situation. In some situations, people are willing and able to work their way through the drama or crisis and move forward.

The relationships we cultivate or not with our siblings or other family members are somewhat different because we most often do not get to pick and choose our family. Most of us tolerate and love them regardless. However, relationships with our friends are intentionally cultivated to a place where we are able to talk about or through any and almost everything—we give one another the hard advice and feedback, even when we know it hurts. We tell friends how we feel without trying to be hurtful. Amid all the technology (telephone, cell phone, email, text-messaging, Twitter, blogging, Facebook, etc.), we still manage to actually talk to our few close friends using some form of verbal communication.

Moreover, as a culture, we have become accustomed to the conveniences of instant gratification—we want everything quick, fast, today, yesterday, or right away. And, with the tickle of a keyboard or keypad from a handheld device, we can have immediate access to information for look-up purposes versus engaging in a healthy dialogue or debating the merits of a situation or issue. Some of us will even send an email to a colleague who sits in the cubicle right next to us instead of getting up out of the chair and walking over to ask a question or engage in dialogue. It's almost as if verbal communication skills are becoming a lost art. Some of us even act as if we have no clue how to engage in a conversation anymore.

Now, I am not sure when it happened, but somewhere along life's journey we as a society and culture arrived at a crossroads in which we stopped talking to our colleagues when it comes to addressing workplace issues. Instead we point fingers, blame someone for our discomfort, and require a third party to intervene for an appropriate resolution—go and straighten someone out. We no longer communicate in either of the most traditional methods, in-person or via telephone. And while almost everyone has a cell phone, the physical telephone call is quickly being replaced by email, text, Twitter, and whatever the next version of these is. Granted our lives are much busier in this era of technology, but in the words of Brooks from the movie *Shawshank Redemption*, "The world done gone and got itself in a hurry overnight." So, we reach for excuses to justify our new and misguided sense of self-importance—"I just don't have enough time to talk right now," "There are just not enough hours in the day," or "I'll do it another time when I have more time." We no longer take time to talk to one another.

Social Networking Media

I recall that prior to the information technology boom when something bothered us or we were put out or put upon about something, we would approach the person and tell them how their behavior made us feel even if it was awkward or came across a little clumsy. Today, many people hide behind a keyboard, keypad, and use email or text-messaging when they want to use words in situations where they cannot seem to find their voice in order to express themselves. Some even break up with their partners via Facebook and other social networking sites, email, or text messages. People use various methods of technology to speak for them. Using social media, email, and text messaging takes away the emotion—we don't have to see the other's reaction. We can break up and not have to see any tears or have a discussion; we can "yell" without any opportunity for the other to respond; we can "edit" things in writing and don't have to be caught off-guard or think on our feet. We say things via text and email that we would never say to a person's face. Even though the communication may be typed or written, words can still hurt—they have tone, emotion, attitude, and expression. Moreover, some people use voice mail when they clearly know the receiving party is not available to answer the phone; and some of us will let it go to voice mail when we don't want to answer.

While we are connected to one another today more than ever before in our history, that connectivity is no longer navigated through the use of oral communications or handwritten letters. According to Turkle (2011), Internet-based social networking sites and text messaging are not only changing the way we interact online, they're straining our personal relationships as well. Turkle's study, which included personal interviews with 300 children and 150 adults, found that people who spend large amounts of their time connecting online are more isolated in their non-virtual lives, leading to emotional disconnection, mental fatigue, and anxiety.

I contend that one example of the cost of this disconnection from each other is road rage. We spend too much time in isolation telecommuting—working from home, obtaining online degrees from the comfort of our keyboards, texting versus talking, framing super-sized emails that nobody wants to read, or on social networking sites versus socially networking. When we get into our cars, we have a tendency to release all of our pent-up frustrations on people we don't know precisely because we have no emotional connection to strangers and it is easy to cower behind a fiberglass frame and power door locks. It's easy to snap on someone who infringes upon us with the smallest infraction using our car—they cut us off, stop short, improperly signal, or drive too slow in the fast lane. We no longer confront one another unless we're hiding behind our keyboard, keypad, or the steering wheel of our cars because it makes us uncomfortable, but not uncomfortable enough to single out a complete stranger. We yell at people in email, break up/end relationships with people on social media websites, or road rage them. Better still, we continue to pay homage to the notion of crafting a new texting dialect that will become universal to everyone in order to decode text messages. Go figure—we no longer have time to spell entire words and will eventually be required to learn this new dialect in order to interpret what is being said.

While communication is central to the evolution of social systems, various communication tools have begun to redefine the manner in which we exchange, interpret, and transfer information and interact online with each other. Several ways in which online social media has revolutionized our means and manner of social communication include:

1. Anyone can reach a global audience twenty-four hours a day, seven days a week.

2. Social media is accessible to anyone at little or no cost.
3. Most anyone can navigate social media sites, which eliminates the need for specialized skills and training.
4. Instantaneous responses between the participants make the communication process extremely reciprocative.
5. Communications can be altered almost instantaneously by comments, editing, voting, and so on.

Some key characteristics of online social communication have posed challenges on the study of social systems in general. The question is—how are online social communication patterns affecting our social lives and our collective behavior today? For example, social websites such as Myspace allows users to post short messages on their friends' profiles, and Facebook allows users to post content on another user's "Wall." These messages are typically short and viewable publicly to the common set of friends to both the users.

Unlike Myspace or Facebook, blogging or tweeting on Twitter takes on a conversational form that provides back-and-forth communication among the users. One of the many disadvantages of social media is that it doesn't allow the user to self-correct for the audience. For example, people write and post things they would never say in front of their parents or grandparents, but their parents or grandparents see it. Do they forget it's visible or is it that they just don't care? Another disadvantage is that it also seems to take away from the person's ability to decide what is and is not relevant or good communication. It gives the "Tweeter" the perception that an active audience awaits word about what he/she had for lunch and can't wait for this tantalizing news. Does this help give a face or personality to the person? Absolutely not! The reality is, while people may know what someone had for lunch, the name of their pet, and the color of their hair, they really are not connecting with them on a personal level.

Moreover, social actions are seen with the recent explosive

growth of popular online communities ranging from picture and video sharing (YouTube.com) and collective music recommendation (Last.fm) to news voting (Digg.com) and social bookmarking (del.icio.us). However, in contrast to traditional communities, these sites do not feature direct communication or conversational mechanisms to its members. There is no return to the communicator and, thus, the ability for feedback is often lost.

We are becoming a culture of nonverbal communication. While technology is a wonderful thing, it is also helping to create a community of incivility. According to a CNN report, Twitter and other social networking tools can possibly numb a person's level of compassion, creating a social morality nightmare where people become indifferent to other people's pain and suffering. We hide behind a keyboard, BlackBerry and cell phone key pad and use written words to express our feelings and tell people off. Hell, we even end relationships (personal as well as professional—terminations and the like) via email, text message, Facebook, and other social networking sites. While technology has its place in our lives, it also has allowed us to cower behind it and use it as an excuse and a weapon to act out publicly and in private. It is now the culprit in shaping how we engage one another, how we treat one another, and how we live amongst one another. We have to stop, slow it down, and turn it around if we're ever going to bridge this great big ole cultural diversity divide we find ourselves in.

In order to bridge the communication gaps we as a society and culture have created and begin to build community with all the diversity amongst us, we have to start allowing people to make mistakes with us. We allow people in our personal lives to make mistakes with us, we talk through it, or work it out; but in the workplace, we can't seem to do the same. We need to be able to talk to one another and risk that our professional relationships can sustain the same type of rigor as our personal ones. People must give others permission to make mistakes with them in order to gain a better understanding of different cultures from a lived perspective. We as a people can't find the recipe in a cookbook— how to be culturally competent in this era of difference; we can't get it from a written prescription from the diversity leader or EEO officer; nor can we get it from a central repository out of the organization's code of conduct or human resources policies and procedures. We have to begin to talk to one another if we're going to take this journey of cultural understanding together and bridge the diversity divide.

Chapter 4

STRATEGIES FOR ADDRESSING S*T*UFF

My Personal Best

As you can see, I'm accustomed to telling my personal story within the context of these sections. I will begin this section with a cultural misstep as a new hire before I introduce you to several strategies that I have used to address this S*t*uff.

Several years ago, I was the successful candidate in a national search for the position as head of the Office of Equal Opportunity for a large university. Prior to my first onsite interview, I received a controversial news article about the office and a student's rights. When I mentioned the article during the interview, I was informed that as a result of the issues raised in the news article along with some others, an external consultant had been commissioned to conduct an assessment of the office that handled the incident. The consultant met with individual leaders, the entire office staff, held focus groups with various constituents (faculty, staff, and students) across the organization, and reviewed the office's internal policies and procedures. This incident began the process of unveiling and unpacking the S*t*uff that had plagued the office and the organization before my arrival.

I was subsequently offered and accepted the position. Prior to my start date, the results from the assessment were submitted to the senior leader in the form of a summary report of findings, which I also received upon my arrival. In addition to the assessment feedback, the human resources leader asked if I would participate in a New Leader Transition (NLT) process. Basically, the NLT process was intended to do four things:

1. Provide a new leader with a significant amount of information from colleagues around critical questions in a short period of time.
2. Provide information in an open and approved process, so there was no fear of reprisal, or appearing disloyal to the previous leadership.
3. Enhance organizational effectiveness during the leadership transition phase.
4. Allow employees a chance to give information to the new leader.

The NLT session included approximately fifty constituents from across the organization. The five questions presented to this group for a response that were most relative to the office as well as my role in it were:

1. What's important or what "really counts" in this office?
2. If you were the new leader, what would you start, stop, or continue doing?
3. What myths, beliefs, or attitudes are helpful or unhelpful to the office?
4. Think about the best experience/interaction/accomplishment/project, etc. you have had with the office. Tell me more about this—why did you choose it?
5. If you arrived at work tomorrow and found that one small thing in the office had changed and made a positive impact, what would it be?

The feedback from the assessment conducted by the external consultant and the NLT were consistent. It was evident that the constituents in the group session had worked very hard at articulating and framing their issues and concerns with the office, the processes, as well as campus perceptions. I have included two tables with this publication—**Table X** compares and contrasts the assessment and the NLT process; and **Table XI** identifies the common themes that resonated throughout both processes.

The feedback from both the assessment and the NLT indicated that the organization's hiring process was not timely and/or transparent. Office functions and operations were not clear or evident. Feedback from all constituents indicated that too many search waivers and exceptions were being approved, and hiring officials were unfairly doling out promotions. Meaning, open positions were not being posted and similarly situated or other qualified employees were not given an equal opportunity to compete. Feedback also indicated that the complaint process was too rigid, complaints were too slow in resolution, and complainants never heard anything from the office as to the outcome. Essentially, there was no follow-up, follow-through, or closure. Some overwhelming feedback indicated that the office advocated for the complainant or one group in particular, blacks/African-Americans. In essence constituents had unpleasant experiences with the office, were uncomfortable raising issues with the office, and never wanted to be summoned to participate in an investigation due to perceptions of guilt or innocence versus how best to resolve the problem. Most troubling was feedback that constituents felt that the process was too punitive and that the office had lost all credibility.

Table X – A Leadership Perspective

A Leadership Perspective

	Assessment	New Leader Transition (NLT)
When	Pre-offer	Post-hire
Why	Events in the organization required a look at diversity issues with specific attention to hiring practices and the complaint process	Quickly provides new leaders with needed critical information from employees to increase organizational effectiveness

Who	• Administration, faculty, staff and students
	• Open forums for interested individuals
	• Review of policies and procedures
		• Faculty, staff and students
		• Affinity groups
		• Constituents from Committees
		   o Women's Advisory Council
		   o Multicultural Center

What	General Observations • Communication • Diversity • The office	1. What counts in the office? 2. Start, stop and continue 3. Myths, beliefs or attitudes 4. Best experience with the Office 5. Small impactful change

Table XI—Common Themes

Assessment Feedback—Common Themes

Communication	Diversity	The Office
• Lack of it	• Awareness of what's been done	• No credibility
• Ineffectiveness		• Lack of timeliness
• Lack of awareness	• Effectiveness	• Hiring and complaint process
• Timeliness	• Overt racism in classes	• Lack of service orientation
• Public v. confidential information	• Differential treatment by student/employee groups by administrative units	• Minimal cooperation with other campus offices
• Mishandling situations		• Rigid complaint procedures
• Lack of transparency	• Minimal/no rep of various social identity groups among faculty/administration	• Guilt or innocence versus fixing problems
	• Lack of communication between social identity groups and university governance groups	• Advocate for complainant
		• Advocate for one specific identity group
	• Crisis management approach to diversity	

While I could have taken this large dose of what tasted like castor oil personally, I decided that while this wasn't about me, it would ultimately fall on my shoulders to fix this Scuff that was plaguing the office. Now, the office had its own brand of Scuff to deal with which was issues constituents across the organization found frustrating. When the follow-up or second meeting was held with the group/participants who provided feedback during the first meeting, my presentation to them was threefold:

1. Because the organization had also recently hired a new diversity leader, all issues related to *diversity* would be referred to that office.
2. While major system changes were required to the online application system and long-term changes to the *hiring processes/practices* required collaboration with human resources, this would be an ongoing work-in-progress. However, as a short-term strategy, the office committed to:

    • Push back and challenge units to conduct open, fair, broad, and competitive searches
    • As a rule we conduct a search and "exceptions" would be rare
    • Require diverse search committees (race/gender) for every search
    • Meet with more search committees on the front-end (kick-off).

Long-term, the office committed to:

    • Develop an online search and screen training module
    • Move service maintenance positions from paper to the online system

- Move faculty applicant monitoring system to a new integrated platform.

3. The complaint process was perceived to be overwhelmingly taxing, and it had its own internal challenges for constituents across the organization. Revamping the *investigation complaint process* using a three-pronged approach versus one perceived to be too rigid and too punitive was the top priority for the office. The three prongs would include:

   i. Consultation and/or facilitated conversations
   ii. Mediation
   iii. Formal Investigation

While feedback from both the assessment and NLT was an outcry for change, I knew that buy-in at the most senior levels of the organization was required if the new approach was going to be successful. This approach required the decisional authority or leader to take ownership of sanctions or any type of perceived reprimand and not the office itself as had been the past practice. Since the office had virtually no jurisdiction over employees, it was better served by relegating the task of doling out or mandating sanctions to the most senior levels of the leadership team.

Within my first ninety days, I was rolling out the details of the three-pronged approach to investigating complaints at the senior leaders' retreat. The overall presentation was based upon my contention that most of the issues being raised in the office were not grounded in illegal harassment or illegal discrimination, but was S*u*ff that was aggravating people, getting on their nerves, or making them sick or tired of a situation. Employees come to the office frustrated about a situation, are unable to articulate their concerns to their supervisor, or have failed to effectively communicate with a colleague as a result of a conflict. So, instead of setting false expectations with the complainants that their Scuff was serious or that someone was going to be fired because of it, the three-pronged approach provided the office with multiple strategies that would more appropriately begin to address the types of issues people were raising.

I consider myself a data person—someone who uses data to make decisions, support or defend a position, or to just make a point. The data I presented at the leadership retreat included current complaint data by individual unit to help sell the merits of the three-pronged approach, the new complaint strategy, and the notion of Scuff. In doing so, however, I stepped in knee-deep all over the organization's cultural toes and learned to never show individual unit data in public. The leaders with the highest number of complaints viewed the data presentation as a poor reflection of their leadership in comparison to those with low complaint numbers. Leaders never want to be made to look bad publicly in front of other leaders, and particularly in front of their boss. Of course, larger units had the biggest numbers of complaints. Who knew someone would go whine back to the most senior leader (my boss) about it. Well, someone did complain to my boss so that he would come back and straighten me out regarding the proper protocols for presenting data in public. As you can see, this Scuff happens at all levels in an organization—even the most senior-level leaders will complain when they're frustrated by someone's behavior. My point here is—now I know better.

While this unfortunately was my first organizational cultural faux pas, fortunately, I lived to tell it. Some of us are allowed to make mistakes in order to better understand or get to know the organizational culture, our colleagues, and the like. I didn't lose my job over it, but I clearly left a sour taste in someone's dessert. In spite of my mishap, after all the relevant reviews for buy-in, the office officially launched the three-pronged approach to investigating complaints and presented this new approach to approximately 500 constituents by the end of the first year of my employ. If you work in an organization long enough, you are going to bump into something or step on something that is offensive to someone else.

Strategies and Approaches for Diffusing Organizational Noise

After spending almost twenty years performing EEO compliance and diversity-related work, I contend that what most people complain about in the workplace is not grounded in illegal harassment or illegal discrimination. It's overwhelmingly S𝒸𝓊ff and they want it fixed or stopped. While I'm not saying that we blow people's issues off, I am saying that we address people's issues using approaches that do not set false expectations about the egregiousness of their issue(s) or that someone will be terminated as a consequence of it. For example, no one is going to get fired because they complimented someone on their outfit and touched the sleeve of the jacket while admiring it. Let's face it—most compliance offices are short-staffed, resource-strapped, and unable to formally investigate every issue that lands at their doorstep. Better yet, let's do some basic math with regard to my current staff dedicated to handle complaints—it is not logical that two people can possibly formally investigate roughly 200 complaints a year. However, these two people can most probably consult and/or facilitate dialogue that more appropriately addresses and diffuses organizational noise that gets mislabeled as harassment or discrimination.

Equal employment opportunity and employee relations professionals do a disservice to employees as well as the organization by allowing complainants to believe that their issues are egregious to the level that someone may actually be in trouble over it. Complainants need to understand that what they describe or present as the issue may not be illegal harassment or illegal discrimination; however, they do need to know that they were heard loud and clear and that their concerns will be worked through to some resolution. They also need to understand that while the matter will have some level of review (look into it, talk to someone, or schedule a meeting and facilitate a conversation), a formal investigation may not be conducted. Now mind you, there will be those occasions when, if any of what's being alleged is remotely true, someone may likely be in trouble (they may need a verbal reprimand, a letter in their personnel file, or stronger sanctions imposed up to and including termination). Most often, my experience in these situations is that this is not the case, that it's S*c*uff." However, we all clearly know when it's not S*c*uff." And in most situations, the complaining party is not attempting to get anyone in trouble; they just want the troublesome behavior to stop.

The office under my leadership currently uses a three-pronged approach to address issues that come into the office: 1) empowerment, consultation, and/or facilitated conversations, which is how approximately 85 percent of the issues are resolved; 2) mediation when relationships need to be salvaged; and 3) formal investigations only when warranted (somebody might be in trouble and need a letter in their personnel file, or other sanctions up to and including suspension, administrative leave, or termination) if what is being alleged is remotely true. With that said, what follows are ten strategies and approaches that may assist you in addressing your S*c*uff.

1. *Empowerment*

Empowerment is the process of enabling or authorizing an individual to think, behave, take action, and control work and decision making in autonomous ways. It is a strategy and philosophy that enables employees to make decisions about their jobs. In this context, this approach enables parties to resolve their own issues and provides them with the tools to progress in their respective relationships. Moreover, it makes parties feel they are or are about to become more in control of their destinies. Heathfield (2000) suggests that the principles of employee empowerment require trust, information sharing, frequent feedback, problem solving, and rewards and recognition that value people, not just in work, but deed.

2. Consultation

In essence, a consultation seeks to build consensus in a manner that unites various constituencies instead of dividing them. It is a discussion aimed at ascertaining opinions or reaching an agreement—a meeting for deliberation, discussion, or decision. It encourages diversity of opinion and acts to control the struggle for power that is otherwise so common in traditional decision-making systems. This approach concentrates on bridging communication gaps. During discussion, participants must make every effort to be as frank and candid as possible, while maintaining a courteous interest in the views of others. Personal attacks, blanket ultimatums, and prejudicial statements are to be avoided. This is an informal process that should not create a heavy paper trail or summary report, but should track the complaint in some type of central data repository. This process can be as confidential or as open as the parties involved choose. Managers or supervisors may not necessarily be involved or even be aware of the issues or conflict unless they are a party to the conflict.

3. Facilitated Conversation

In my experience, a hybrid of empowerment, consultation, and/or facilitated conversation has been used in my office to address most of the Scuff. Similar to mediation, a facilitated conversation uses an objective, non-judgmental facilitator to help individuals listen to one another and move toward a resolution.

Facilitated conversations are confidential and are focused on problem solving with a mutually agreed-upon outcome. An assessment of the issue presented should determine whether a facilitated conversation with relevant parties is an appropriate means to resolve the matter. Tips for getting the most out of a facilitated conversation can be found in **Appendix C.**

Facilitation can play an important role in ensuring a well-run dialogue or engagement process. Useful facilitation skills include planning agendas, creating the appropriate group environment, encouraging participation, and leading the group to reach its objectives. Effective facilitators balance their focus along three dimensions:

1. Outcomes/Goals—the facilitator is attempting to get to a particular outcome or end.
2. Process/How—the facilitator is concerned about how to get to the aim, paying attention to the quality of the process. For instance, the facilitator doesn't want to make all decisions or do all the talking; but at the same time, the facilitator is concerned about the flow, efficiency, and ease of the process.
3. Inclusion/People—the facilitator has to be aware of and observant about the individuals' and group's behavior and participation, attempting to reaffirm and trust participants' contributions.

Steve Davis, life coach and infopreneur, suggests five guidelines for effectively facilitating group conversations:

1. Get everyone involved because people often politely allow others to monopolize the conversation or will tolerate a tirade when they're clearly uncomfortable speaking up. In situations such as these, the facilitator should validate the speaker, and then ask for input from the other party.

2. When appropriate, it's okay to interrupt in order to redirect the dialogue. While listening is an important skill as a facilitator, people who talk too much or who talk over others expect to be interrupted because it's the only way they really get to engage in an actual dialogue.

3. Ensure you are actively listening because good dialogue or conversations require us to stay present and pay attention to what's being said. Meaning, we don't entertain other thoughts and allow our minds to wander while we're listening. Bring the focus back to the speaker.

4. Stay on track, but be willing to leave it. Sometimes conversations can be all over the place, and tend to be going someplace but haven't arrived yet. When this occurs, be flexible and willing to move from one subject or idea to another, but be aware of unfinished ideas or thoughts that are left hanging. This most often occurs when poor listening skills or constant interruptions on the part of someone disrupts the flow of dialogue.

5. Work on cultivating your relationships—we need to work on relating better to one another. Start by asking yourself how you would like to be related to, then "walk the walk."

Some types of issues or Stuff in which a hybrid of empowerment, consultation, and/or facilitated conversation approach was used have been human resources-related issues (attendance, suspension, termination, performance, etc.). In most cases, the employee had already raised the issue with HR but did not like the outcome, so they reframed it as harassment or discrimination in order to get another review. And if that doesn't work, they may take it further (EEOC, OCR, or lawyer up). Most of this Stuff also includes messy conflicts within the department, issues of favoritism, as well as mishaps, missteps, misunderstandings, or miscommunications based on perceptions. The same also applies to faculty who may have previously raised their issues through the faculty grievance process and didn't like the outcome. Students tend to raise issues regarding something a faculty member said during class, a comment made in class by another student, a grade, a paper, and the like. Students will also shop their issues across campus until they get the outcome they're looking for (dean's office, ombudsperson, advisors, student affairs office, OCR, etc.).

While most of the issues that come into the office are clearly not bona fide complaints of discrimination or harassment, the office will make every attempt to resolve the matter. Now remember, once an employee seeks an external resource outside the unit or department for resolution, they are way beyond issues at the level of the toilet paper roll. And while most small infractions in the workplace are not necessarily illegal harassment or illegal discrimination, it is still Scuff that they want stopped.

Let me give you a few examples. An employee raised allegations of harassment asserting that the supervisor "yelled" at him in an email—this is Scuff. Another employee raised concerns about issues regarding fair treatment and what she could only describe as bullying behavior. She asserted that race or gender was not a factor, but wanted the bullying behavior stopped. The employee had concerns about attempts to push her out of the organization before she had another position and requested a consultation to discuss her concerns, strategies on how to handle her situation, and an assessment of other alternatives and possible options—this is Scuff.

A black employee alleged discrimination based on his race because he did not receive a salary increase with a lateral transfer, whereas his white coworker did receive a salary increase with a lateral transfer. A review of the salary data revealed that the black employee was the highest paid supervisor, and he believed that because he had more seniority he should have been paid more. A review of salary data also indicated that new hires were traditionally compensated at the same rate as current employees. In the case of lateral transfers, the records did not reflect any employee receiving a salary increase with the exception of the white coworker, in which case there appeared to be a significant difference between the two employees' salaries. In order to achieve parity, the white coworker received a salary increase. The evidence obtained through this salary review did not support the allegation of discrimination on the basis of race because it appeared to be standard business practice to compensate employees at the same salary regardless of their employment history. The primary objective was to achieve parity among the staff. For example, all things being equal, had another employee (also black) been given the position, they, too, would have received the salary increase to establish parity—this is S*uff.

4. Mediation

Mediation is for parties that want to save the relationship. Mediation is used as an intervention to work with two or more parties to help them reach a mutually agreed-upon resolution that usually involves compromise. Parties usually seek out mediation because they are ready to work toward a resolution to their dispute. The very fact that parties are willing to mediate in most circumstances means that they are ready to "move" on their S*uff. Since both parties are willing to work toward resolving the case, they are more likely to work toward resolution and reach compromise than against one another.

When issues are raised in the office, an investigator will assess the situation to determine whether mediation is appropriate. Either the complainant or the respondent may refuse mediation or, once commenced, end mediation at any time. No adverse inference is drawn from any such decision. The parties involved in the mediation session are provided with the relevant notifications and acknowledgments. Mediation must be mutually acceptable to both parties.

Moreover, the process of mediation represents a commitment on the part of all parties to resolve the matter with a signed agreement of the terms and conditions of the resolution. In mediation, the parties have control over the resolution, and the resolution can be unique to the dispute. Often, solutions developed by the parties are ones that a judge, jury, or other arbitrator could not provide. Thus, mediation is more likely to produce a result that is mutually agreeable, or win/win, for the parties. And because the result is attained by the parties working together and is mutually agreeable, the compliance with the mediated agreement is usually high. During the past five years, my office mediated eighteen issues; 89 percent of the mediated cases resulted in the relationship enduring one year or longer past mediation, whereas 11 percent (two) of the cases were the result of a failure to cooperate.

A mediator must be impartial. The mediator, as a neutral, gives no legal advice, but guides the parties through the problem-solving process. The mediator may or may not suggest alternative solutions to the dispute. Whether he or she offers advice or not, the trained mediator helps the parties think "outside of the box" for possible solutions to the dispute, thus enabling the parties to find the avenue to dispute resolution that suits them best. A mediator is assigned to the case who will schedule and conduct the mediation session. If mediation is successful, the complainant and the respondent will sign a mediation agreement, and the matter will be considered resolved. Both parties are reminded of their obligation to comply with the agreement. If mediation is not feasible, or is not successful within a reasonable period of time, the office may commence with a formal investigation.

Mediation has a structure unlike that of a facilitated conversation. Specifically, the process is private and confidential. It's like Vegas; whatever happens in mediation stays in mediation, remaining strictly confidential. No one but the parties to the dispute and the mediator(s) know what has gone on in the mediation. The only exceptions to such strict confidentiality would involve child abuse or actual or threatened criminal acts. Confidentiality in mediation, including in the workplace, has such significance that in most cases the legal system cannot force a mediator to testify in court as to the content of what occurred in mediation. And, many mediators will destroy their notes once the dispute is resolved.

One of the greatest benefits of mediation is that it allows people to resolve the charge in a friendly way and in ways that meet their own unique needs. Also, a complaint or charge can be resolved faster through mediation. While it takes less than three months on average to resolve a charge through mediation, it can take six months or longer for a complaint or charge to be investigated. Mediation is fair, efficient, and can help the parties avoid a lengthy investigation and litigation.

Federal agencies are required to have an alternative dispute resolution program. Most use mediation, but not necessarily the EEOC process. With the EEOC's Mediation Process, shortly after a charge is filed, the agency may contact both the employee and employer to ask if they are interested in participating in mediation. The decision to mediate is completely voluntary. If either party turns down mediation, the charge will be forwarded to an investigator. If both parties agree to mediate, a mediation session is scheduled which is conducted by a trained and experienced mediator. If the parties do not reach an agreement at the mediation, the charge will be investigated like any other charge. A written signed agreement reached during mediation is enforceable in court just like any other contract.

Not long ago, I mediated a session with two members of the leadership team in the same unit that was suffering from some major communication challenges. Three key issues were evident after the first two-hour session: 1) the junior leader was misreading conversations, unable to articulate concerns verbally, and not sharing content and details; 2) perceptions that the senior leader did not listen and was not providing their undivided attention during meetings; and 3) the two leaders never engaged in impromptu conversations or discussions of any kind. While there was a litany of actionable behavioral changes required on both their parts, the most notable that were included in the mediation agreement were: 1) the junior leader agreed to write out details prior to scheduled meetings, whereas the senior leader agreed to probe for additional information when unclear; 2) both agreed to try to hear what was being said and not get caught up in the words; and 3) both agreed to not send nonessential or non-critical email to one another for a period of six weeks—they agreed to get up from their desk and engage in face-to-face conversations. While I would like for you to believe that these actions totally resolved their communication challenges, that would be misleading. In the next scheduled follow-up session, the list of actionable behavioral changes slightly grew. Consequently, the original mediation agreement was appended to include the additional behavioral changes, and the two eventually reached a plateau in which they were able to communicate at some level.

5. *Formal Investigation*

A formal investigation occurs when what's being alleged would be a policy violation or a violation of EEO laws and statutes, if remotely true. In these cases, somebody may be in trouble and require due process to the greatest extent of the law and organizational practices. This includes a comprehensive investigative approach. In these cases, the office will make a determination on the classification of the complaint as well as a preliminary assessment that the issues raised warrant a formal investigation. The office will provide official written notification to the relevant parties and decisional authority, as appropriate. If a need for immediate interim action is determined (e.g., removal, reassignment, administrative leave, or suspension), such actions will be administered by the decisional authority. The investigator will conduct fact-finding through interviews with the complainant, the respondent, and any other witnesses identified by either party, along with an examination of written statements from the parties, supporting documentation, and any other relevant evidence. The investigator will identify provisions of applicable policies that may have been violated if the allegations prove more likely true than not.

Witnesses, including the complainant and the respondent, may have counsel at their scheduled interviews, but counsel will not be allowed to participate in the interview and may be asked to leave the interview site if disruptive. Finally, if a complainant or respondent's counsel is present at the interview, counsel for the organization will also be present.

All members of the organization are required to cooperate fully with the investigative process. The decisional authority is responsible for approving any disciplinary or remedial measures recommended by the office and for notifying the complainant and respondent of the decision and what, if any, disciplinary or remedial measures may be imposed or implemented.

6. *Alternate Dispute Resolution (ADR)*

Alternate dispute resolution typically refers to any means of settling disputes outside of litigation that can include early neutral evaluation, negotiation, conciliation, mediation, arbitration, and collaborative law. The two most commonly used forms of ADR are arbitration and mediation. Some ADR programs are voluntary, while others are mandated by the courts. Specifically, courts require some parties to engage in mediation before permitting their cases to be heard.

7. *Negotiation*

Negotiation is a discussion between two or more parties who are trying to work out a solution to a problem that neither one could do on their own (Maiese 2003). While negotiation usually involves a process of give and take if a settlement is to be reached, the existence of a conflict of interest between them requires the use of some form of influence to get a better deal, rather than simply taking what the other side is offering. The parties prefer to search for agreement rather than fight openly, give in, or break off dialogue. While they have interlocking goals that they cannot accomplish independently, they usually do not want or need exactly the same thing. This interdependence can lead to either win-lose or win-win resolutions.

There are primarily two strategies for negotiating: 1) interest-based (or integrative or cooperative); and 2) positional (or distributive or competitive). In their best-selling book on negotiation, *Getting to Yes,* Roger Fisher and William Ury argue that there are three approaches: hard, soft, and what they call "principled negotiation." Hard is essentially extremely competitive bargaining; soft is extremely integrative bargaining (so integrative that one gives up one's own interests in the hopes of meeting the other person's interests); and principled negotiation is supposed to be somewhere in between, but closer to soft, certainly, not hard.

8. *Intergroup Dialogue*

By dialogue, I am referring to a specific form of communication especially designed to help people communicate across social, cultural, and power differences. The goal in dialogue is to work toward understanding, not necessarily to reach agreement. While the purpose of intergroup dialogue is often expressed as "education for social justice," among other goals it is hoped that groups will increase their understanding of each other; use this understanding to honestly and deeply explore differences in privilege and discrimination between groups; and ask themselves what next steps, if any, they wish to take to promote equality.

1. Intergroup dialogues are carefully structured face-to-face meetings between members of at least two social groups. For example, dialogue might occur between the following groups:

   - Women and men
   - People of color and white people
   - African-Americans and Latino/as
   - Lesbian, gay, bisexual, transgendered persons, and heterosexuals
   - Asian-Americans of different ethnicities
   - Persons of different socioeconomic classes/status
   - Native Americans and other U.S. citizens
   - Recent immigrants and older immigrants
   - Persons with disabilities and able-bodied persons

2. The groups are co-facilitated by at least two people, one from each social group. Facilitators have been well trained in the specific techniques of dialogue.

   - Facilitators must be experienced in the ongoing processes of exploring their own attitudes and behaviors regarding diversity and social justice.
   - Training should enable them to create safe environments where participants can discuss difficult topics with honesty.
   - They should know how to share power and create democratic, non-authoritarian environments.
   - They should be trained in expert listening skills and in empathy skills.

3. The number of participants is typically fourteen to sixteen people—small enough to encourage and permit each participant to have a voice and be heard, yet large enough to access diversity within and between the groups.

4. The participants commit in advance to participate in dialogue over a sustained period of time—ideally over ten to fourteen meetings (although dialogues of four to five meetings have also been conducted).

5. Dialogues may be conducted in academic settings like high schools and universities, and they can also occur in other settings such as churches, community centers, businesses, clubs, homes, etc.

Intergroup dialogue participants are encouraged to take a critical perspective when examining how relationships among groups are shaped and affected by the dynamics of interpersonal, institutional and societal power, privilege, and exclusion. Dialogue participants are also challenged to make meaning of the various forms of information introduced in the dialogue through sustained engagement that embraces thoughts and feelings, self-reflection, perspective taking, and critical reflection. Hence, the dialogic dimension of intergroup dialogue challenges participants to be mindful, involved, responsive, and willing to explore contentious issues in collaborative ways. Source: www.igr.umich.edu

9. Civil Discourse

Civil discourse is an engagement in conversation intended to enhance understanding. According to Gergen (2001), civil discourse is the language of dispassionate objectivity and requires respect of the other participants. It neither diminishes the other's moral worth, nor questions his or her good judgment; it avoids hostility, direct antagonism, or excessive persuasion; it requires modesty and an appreciation for the other participant's experiences even during challenging and uncomfortable conversations. Demeaning comments or speech or actions that harass or discriminate on the basis of race, color, ethnicity, age, gender, religion, national origin, disability, or sexual orientation should not be tolerated.

According to Brown (2011), Calvin Davis' book, *In Defense of Civility*, makes the persuasive argument that civility begins with each of us and that there are clear, defining characteristics for what makes for civil discourse about the great moral issues facing us. Davis defines civility as "the exercise of patience, integrity, humility, and mutual respect in civil conversation, even [or especially] with those with whom we disagree." Brown contends that we must learn patience and hear our neighbor's position in his or her own voice. In short, we have to listen to those who disagree with us. This means fact-checking our own assertions as well as those of our opponents. Humility requires that "we enter every public conversation open to the possibility that we could change our minds" (Brown). Mutual respect means "honoring each other's right to represent moral worldviews in public and avoiding demonizing one another. It requires that, even if I think you are tragically mistaken, I honor your right to participate in the American enterprise of public moral conversation" (Brown). It is a good place for all of us to begin the arduous and necessary task of rediscovering how to engage one another in civil discourse about race, class, social justice, and other issues that demand our best ethical and moral reflection.

Somehow, we have lost the ability to agree to disagree in a way that shows respect for the other person's point of view, even if we don't agree with their beliefs. There are better, more productive ways to discuss issues and arrive at a solution that addresses the needs of everyone involved. Civil discourse "is our ability to have conversation about topics about which we disagree, and our ability to listen to each other's perspectives" (Brown).

The CivilityProject is an organization initiated due to the alarming and increasingly vicious tone in American politics and society. The CivilityProject published "Nine Rules of Civil Discourse" to guide behavior that directs us toward positive resolution of issues we face. These nine rules require that we:

1. Show respect—honor other people and their opinions, especially in the midst of a disagreement.
2. Pay attention—be aware and attend to the world and the people around you.
3. Listen—focus on others in order to better understand their point of view.
4. Be inclusive—welcome all groups of people working for the greater good of the community.
5. Don't gossip and don't accept it when others choose to do so.
6. Be agreeable—look for opportunities to agree. Don't contradict just to do so.
7. Apologize—be sincere and repair damaged relationships.
8. Give constructive criticism—when disagreeing, stick to the issues and don't make a personal attack.
9. Take responsibility—don't shift responsibility and blame to others; share disagreements publicly.

Source: CivilityProject.org—http://www.harvestmoon.coop/forms/nine_rules.pdf

10. Democracy Plaza

Democracy plaza is both a chalkboard structure and an active student organization. The democracy plaza structure consists of three large chalkboard structures on which the democracy plaza student organization posts weekly thought-provoking questions regarding local, national, and global issues. Visitors to the boards can respond to the questions using the chalk provided, and questions are changed weekly to reflect current topics. The area enclosed by the democracy plaza chalkboards is used as a programming space and hosts a diversity of events that are organized by both the democracy plaza student organization and other campus groups.

Democracy plaza is a space made available for student groups, professors, staff, and others to reserve and use as a platform for deep and sometimes difficult discussions about society. It provides campus communities with "an opportunity to express, speak, and hear diverging thoughts surrounding social, political, economic, and religious issues relevant to the campus, city, state, country, and world. Its mission supports the development of well-informed and engaged students through critical thinking and civil discourse on political ideas and issues."

Source: http://life.iupui.edu/osi/civic-engagement/political/dp.html

Overcoming Cultural Missteps

Somehow our diversity has become the divide. In order to bridge the communication gaps we as a society and culture have created and begin to build community, we have to allow people to make some mistakes with us. Unfortunately, we cannot become culturally competent through shared and lived experiences without stepping on toes, bumping into someone's culture, and being forgiven for those missteps and mishaps. We manage to allow people in our personal lives to make mistakes with us—we forgive a crass "joke," we talk through it and work it out. But, for some reason, we cannot seem to extend the same courtesies when it comes to our colleagues in the workplace. We hold a grudge over unintentional slights such as leaving a team member off an email, or misspoken or insensitive words. We need to be able to talk to one another and take some risks, knowing that our professional relationships can sustain the same type of rigor as our personal ones without fear of retribution, complaints, litigation, etc. While our collective workplace cultures may dictate stricter limits on gaining personal knowledge about people's culture and background, when taking those risks, we must give our colleagues permission to misstep in order to gain a better understanding of one another's culture and background from a shared perspective.

Again, there are no sure-fire recipes on how to be culturally competent in a society of difference. The EEO officer or diversity leader can't write you a prescription. Nor can you get it from the archives of human resources operating policies, procedures, and practices, or the student code of conduct rule book. In fact, these would probably do more to constrict understanding. The preceding chapter provided some strategies and approaches for diffusing organizational noise—navigating through the messy missteps, mishaps, misunderstanding, and miscommunications of social and organizational behavior. Each and every situation or incident alleged, while similar, will have its own unique nuances and its own individual series of steps to reach resolution. However, if we're going to take the journey of cultural understanding together, we as a people need to get out more often socially and talk to one another. At the end of the day, *it's time to talk through this S***ff.* What follows are some strategies and approaches that may assist you in addressing your own S***ff.

- Give people permission to make mistakes with you, whether they misstep, misspeak, or even misunderstand. Reflect on the last time you misstepped and recall how you felt when the person forgave your transgression.
- Take some risks and get to know one person that you don't know and embrace the journey knowing it's not life ending. We are all going to make mistakes with one another, so learn the lesson and turn the page on it.
- Ask people for permission to make mistakes with them,

especially people from other ethnic, cultural, and international backgrounds that you are most likely to be unfamiliar with.

- Identify and strip away stereotypes and myths about groups that may generally be regarded as different from groups with which you have an affinity.
- Build authentic and significant relationships with people who may be regarded as different in order to acquire an understanding of the issues created by group differences.
- Examine and learn how to listen for the assumptions that may drive the differences in the perceptions and perspectives of others.

Rubs have their roots in cultural norms

The objective in dealing with your own Scuff should not be to try to censor or interpret everything people say, looking for some underlying meaning, or examining what they do, looking to pass judgment because we find the action unbecoming. What we should be working toward is engaging in open and candid dialogue and becoming capable of functioning effectively in the context of our differences. The objective of cultural competence is not to assimilate women, minorities, and other groups into the dominant culture, but rather to create different heterogeneous cultures in the dominant culture's place, making a shared environment where employees can adapt or adjust their approach to compensate for the cultural differences.

There are organizational and personal benefits to be gained by dealing with the Scuff.

Organizational benefits include:

- Reduced stress in the unit
- Reduced turnover

- Increased productivity and efficiency
- Increased morale and cooperation within teams and groups
- Maximized profits and improved customer service
- Reduced lawsuits and agency charges

Individual benefits include:

- Performance potential is improved
- Increased promotion potential
- Gain cooperation from others
- Organizational influence will increase
- Ability to set priorities
- Colleagues will respect what you do

If Scuff is left unresolved, it can be pretty costly. First, it can interfere with the organization's ability to meet customer needs by providing timely, quality products and/or services. Secondly, when Scuff is left unresolved in a manner acceptable to all parties, time and other valuable resources are wasted, and people get frustrated and either quit trying or quit their jobs altogether. In addition, animosity develops, coworkers stop cooperating, information is withheld in power struggles, and the entire organization suffers as a result. Lastly, conflicts involving value differences can result in poor decisions, missed opportunities, stress, personal illness, absenteeism—poor time and attendance, lower profits, and poor customer service.

Chapter 5

GETTING DOWN TO BRASS TACTICS

Can We Just Talk About It?

The process of communicating between two people consists of transmitting and receiving information. It is only when both parties are performing both tasks effectively and has the same rules can there be effective communication. This sounds relatively simple, but in reality, it is difficult for most people. While people may be attempting to listen to what's being said, their body language, emotions that show up via their tone, the volume of the conversation which sounds like a loud noise, and their attitude all have a tendency to get in the way of effective communication. The most serious communication challenges in personal interactions are due to feelings, but it is those feelings that are also the most important aspect of communication.

Transmission

Everyone needs other people with whom to share their thoughts, ideas, feelings, experiences, problems, and needs. In order to share, they must transmit information or some type of message—good, bad, or indifferent. Efficient transmitters can share themselves, especially feelings, with other people freely and without static (body language, attitude, emotions, or noise), distortion, or interference. Transmission doesn't work when:

- transmitters are not aware of the messages they are sending.
- multiple or conflicting messages are being sent.
- messages are transmitted in some code, slang, dialect, or language that the receiver does not understand.
- the real message is disguised, expressed indirectly, or hidden within a message.
- transmitters communicate too much information.

Reception

Crystal-clear reception of a transmission occurs when the receiver can replay the entire message back to the transmitter's satisfaction. While transmitters may think their message has been clearly articulated, this often is not the case because much of what gets communicated are feelings and emotions that distort the original reception. Good reception requires a concentrated effort and attention to listening or thinking with the speaker instead of concentrating on preparing a response or rebuttal to what is being said. Most often, people do not actually listen to one another because they are constantly interrupting mid-sentence or both are attempting to talk at the same time and one ends up talking over the other. Instead of listening, they are thinking about themselves, they are getting ready for what they'll say next, or they are thinking about the other person (how boring, how stupid, how they wish they would just stop talking, or how they are not buying anything this person is saying). Hence, these missed opportunities to communicate, which form the basis of misunderstandings, culminate into what we see as the messy mishaps and missteps of social and organizational behaviors.

Crystal-clear reception can be particularly difficult when people are simultaneously transmitting messages verbally and nonverbally. A great deal of nonverbal communication occurs, particularly body language, when people are together. In these situations reception is lost because the transmitters may be unaware of the nonverbal transmissions, the verbal and nonverbal messages may appear contradictory, or the receivers ignore or misinterpret the nonverbal signals. Moreover, transmitting and receiving become even more challenging when risk is factored into the situation. Risk comes into play when transmitters are transmitting to and about the receiver. More specifically, when a person transmits something they are uncomfortable with such as feedback, criticism, love, anger, hurt, disgust, or the like, the task of transmitting becomes more challenging.

If a transmitter fears the receiver's reactions, crystal-clear transmission becomes even harder. And, if the receiver demonstrates that they are at all threatened, things can become even more difficult and can result in conflict. It is one thing for the receiver to offer understanding and acceptance when the transmitter is talking about other things and other people. However, it is totally different when the transmitter starts talking about the receiver and about their feelings toward them, especially negative ones. The receiver may feel attacked; thus the need to defend themselves, run away or retreat, or retaliate by attacking the transmitter. It is at this point that one of the parties may bring the issue forward in the workplace, not as a failed attempt to communicate, but as illegal harassment or illegal discrimination. He or she will be way past the level of the toilet paper roll and looking for someone else to fix it, straighten somebody out, stop some behavior, and communicate for them.

While many relationships break down at this point, the results can be amazing if individuals stay with it and continue their efforts to communicate. Communication often breaks down because participants are frustrated, anxious, and discouraged. They say "To hell with it!" and give up. In other words, when we hear information that comes to us, we diagnose it using our own cultural lenses to make notations of what we view as applicable, and then act or respond. It is not that people do not want to hear what we have to say; it is how we are trying to say it that they do not want to hear. If people can remove all the static that gets in the way of effective communication, they can then hear each other. Unless or until the static is removed so two people can continue to work together and communicate, the Scuff in the workplace will remain unresolved—the organizational noise will stay at a very high level.

Communication noise set us up for miscommunications, misunderstandings, missteps, and mishaps because the receiver is unable to comprehend the message being sent or inadvertently misconstrues it. And, because the receiver heard what's being said doesn't mean they understand it or agree with it. In the static model **(Table XII)**, several interferences (body language, attitude, emotions, and noise) hinder the receiver from decoding the message being sent. A receiver will disconnect, check out, or shut down when the static in a conversation reaches a level that makes them uncomfortable. What follows are examples of several types of communication noise that create ineffective transmission:

- Organizational noise in the form of poorly structured communication can prevent the receiver from accurate interpretation. For example, unclear and poorly articulated instructions can make the receiver even more confused about an assignment.
- Syntactical noise is as simple as mistakes in grammar that can disrupt and create distractions in communication, such as abrupt changes in verb tense during a sentence or poorly written messages laden with errors and typos.
- Cultural noise is stereotypical assumptions and perceptions about other groups that can cause misunderstandings, such as unintentionally offending a non-Christian person by wishing them a "Merry Christmas" or saying "bless you" when someone sneezes.

- Psychological noise involving certain attitudes can also make communication difficult. For instance, visible anger, open hostility, or sadness may cause someone to lose focus on what's being said in the moment.
- Environmental noise physically disrupts communication, such as standing next to loudspeakers at a party, or the noise from a construction site next to a classroom making it difficult to hear the professor.
- Physiological impairment noise—physical maladies can prevent effective communications such as actual deafness or blindness that can prevent messages from being received as they were intended. Autism, ADD/ADHD, bipolar disorder, and depression may also severely hamper effective communication.
- Semantic noise is the different interpretations of the meanings of certain words. For example, the word "weed" can be interpreted as an undesirable plant in a yard, as a euphemism for marijuana, or as the process of elimination (weed out the undesirables or unqualified).

If effective communication is ever going to see the light of day by bridging communication gaps, senders and receivers will have to seek to understand each other by listening to what's being said; showing respect by hearing one another out; refraining from being judgmental; and trying to see the other's point of view. What I am saying is that we need to try not to get caught up on the words people use, but instead try to listen to the meaning of what's being said and the story that's being told. There are a myriad of approaches to addressing people's Scuff frivolous or not.

Table XII – Static Model

Static Model

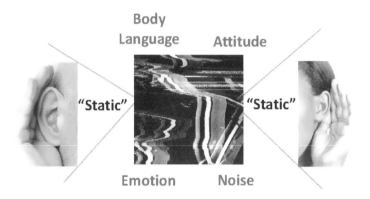

Body Language   Attitude

"Static"   "Static"

Emotion   Noise

While people may be attempting to listen to what's being said, body language, emotions that show up via tone and volume of the conversation, attitude as well as noise has a tendency to get in the way of effective communication.

Where Do We Go From Here?

Let me say this again in case you did not hear me the first time. Today more than ever, when someone steps on someone else's culture, history, beliefs, value system, customs, or traditions, we as a society and a people cry foul—we want some visual and public sanction imposed. We contend that they should have known better. We expect our business, professional, and political leaders to be politically correct and culturally competent. Yet, most people are so afraid of being politically incorrect or culturally insensitive (saying the wrong thing, making the wrong choice, doing the wrong thing, or making a bad decision) that they have become paralyzed in place. As evidenced by some of the most highly publicized social and political faux pas that have had

life-changing consequences for some of the nation's most promi-
nent leaders and media personalities, almost any and everything
is offensive these days. Hence, people become reluctant to weigh
in via commentary, speak up or out on an issue, or take any type
of action as it may be perceived as controversial. Inaction is not
a strategy.

Regardless of the type of organizational structure or unit,
people will raise issues in and outside the organization. Some will
lawyer up, some run to local and national media outlets for sen-
sational purposes and maximum exposure, and some reach for a
third-party intervention. Some employees are barely on speaking terms with each other, which further perpetuates a person's
inability to engage in any type of conversation or civil dialogue
that begins to sort through the messy mishaps of organizational
behavior.

I don't profess to have all the right answers; nor are they written in these pages. However, what I have spent the last 100 pages
talking about is how we as members of the broader community—professionals and leaders in community-based, non-profit,
higher education as well as public and private organizations—can
begin to change the way we look at issues raised as harassment
and discrimination. Simply because people label their issues as
such, doesn't legitimize it as such. Likewise, just because they
don't label it as such, doesn't mean that it isn't a bona fide claim
of harassment or discrimination either.

Coming Full Circle

Martha Stewart went to jail for lying under oath about a
stock trade, but Paula Deen was publicly condemned for telling
the truth about using the "N" word thirty years ago. As you can
see, the truth won't set you free. Paula Deen gave a videotaped
deposition as part of a discrimination suit she was facing in which
she discussed her desire to have a "very southern-style wedding"

for her brother modeled after a restaurant where the "whole entire waitstaff was middle-aged black men" clad in white jackets and black bow ties. While Deen denied telling racial jokes, she acknowledged using the "N word" during a very different time in American history. Deen says she probably used the racial slur when she told her husband about an incident where a black man came into the bank that she was working at and put a gun to her head, which did not leave her feeling real favorable toward the robber.

Consequently, public outcry forced her corporate supporters to withdraw all advertising and endorsements, including cancellation of her show on the Food Network. Even today, we do not forgive missteps, mistakes, and transgressions, but rather would have Paula Deen stripped of all her earning power so that her debt can be "paid in full" to society. However, public opinion was split over corporate's heavy-handed sanctions in response to the Paula Deen incident. As a result, I will leave you with one final story about how the controversy played out in my circle of friends.

The last weekend in June, a longtime friend of mine visited my home for a few days. The weekend was filled with two social engagements in which the Paula Deen incident took center stage. The first discussion took flight at a happy hour that Friday evening; and the second discussion was still running on full throttle at a wine tasting that Saturday evening. A third discussion occurred five days later amid the open flames during a cookout on the fourth of July.

It is almost a blur about how the topic of Paula Deen was introduced during the happy hour. However, early into the discussion, I found myself embroiled in a spirited debate (with a woman I will refer to as Diane) over the corporate sanctions Deen experienced for admitting under oath that she used the "N" word thirty years ago. First, I must say that Diane has a very loose relationship with the "N" word and floated it into just about every other sentence she used. Now mind you, I had to address it and informed her that I was very offended with her use of the word and asked that she not use it in my presence because I don't like the word, don't use the word, nor did I grow up using the word in any context. I went on to say that my intent was not to censor her, but to inform the people I spend time around how I feel about the word, and I would appreciate it if she could exercise some restraint in my presence. While Diane acknowledged my feelings, she continued to slip and slide around the "N" word while arguing that Paula Deen got what she deserved for using the very same word she could not seem to remove from her vocabulary. At the end of this spirited dialogue, which lasted about forty minutes, the position I took was this—until black people stop using the "N" word, Paula Deen gets a pass for something she said thirty years ago.

The next day, my girlfriend and I attended a wine tasting that rotates between various homes every other month. I must confess that anytime this group of women congregates, it's always in the kitchen and around food. There were eight of us hovering over a cheese board with crackers and a fruit tray when the Paula Deen question surfaced. Someone asked, "What do y'all think about Paula Deen?" "Again?" I commented. You guessed right—this dialogue took center stage and turned out to be more spirited than the one the night before. However, I almost passed completely out when one woman stated that she refers to her teenage daughters using the "N" word and provided examples for the context that she used it in. Most of the women argued that Paula Deen got what she deserved for using the "N" word and her desire to plan a wedding for her brother where all the servers are black men in white jackets and black bow ties, similar to the Jim Crow era. However, a few of us argued that what happened to Paula had nothing to do with her use of the "N" word thirty years ago, but rather was corporate's attempt to do damage control in anticipation of public outcry from the black community. While some of us believe corporate overreacted and imposed extreme sanctions for a comment that was thirty years old, others found the actions to be exemplary of social justice. While we all wholeheartedly debated the merits of the Deen incident from our varying perspectives, again, I had to get on my soapbox and address it. I intently and adamantly informed my girlfriends that I am personally very offended with the use of the "N" word and that just because I'm black doesn't mean I'm okay with the word, nor does it give them permission to use the word with me. I don't like the word, I don't use the word, nor did I grow up using the word when I communicate with people. I need people to understand how I feel about their use of the word in my presence and to respect that. My girlfriend who was visiting commented, "What you all really don't know is that she is serious about that and means it." While a couple of the women acknowledged my feelings, they also continued to slip and slide around the word during the evening and would laugh recognizing they misstepped because I would throw up my hands in frustration and say, "What is that?" That was S*c*uff that I found frustrating. However, I continued to hold on to the position that until black people stop using the "N" word, Paula Deen gets a pass.

Who knew that this comment would spark another twenty minutes of spirited dialogue about a double standard for black people who profess they feel outraged, offended, and injured when white people use the "N" word, but will use it during conversations similar to what I was hearing that evening, in reference to other black people and each other, and as one woman admitted, in reference to her daughters. To use one of my most frequent expressions—"Who does that?" It is foolish for black folks to think that the "N" word is actually a term of endearment.

A couple of the women in their mid-thirties took the position that their children will be desensitized to the "N" word because of their lack of exposure to the word and how it is used today. Again, black folks and their foolishness—who does that? I responded that they are truly naïve and in denial if they believe that their children will not experience any negative impact when the "N" word is directed toward them regardless of whether it comes from a white person or a black person. Bull crap! Not quite the words I used, but some of you get my point.

This brings me to the capstone dialogue that occurred at a cookout on the fourth of July. I don't need to say much more except that the conversation, however it surfaced, continued in the same vein as the others. However, this dialogue also included the black male perspective, which was not the case with the other two. It was refreshing to hear a young brother in his late twenties admit that the "N" word was part of his vocabulary growing up. However, after he married and had children, he could no longer rationalize why he was using the word whether it was with the "a" or the "er." As he matured, he no longer reached for the "N" word to express himself because he wanted to be a role model for his children. I suddenly had a sense of pride and felt somewhat vindicated to know that not all of our young black people are lost in some misguided sense that the "N" word with an "a" is actually a term of endearment.

Deen was born sixty years ago when America's South had segregated schools, separate restrooms, different restaurants, and blacks and whites rode in different sections of the bus. Deen made a mistake thirty years ago and refused to make another mistake by lying about it. Likened to the young brother in the scenario above, Deen says that the "N" word is not a word that she has used as time has gone on; things have changed since the sixties in the South, and she and her family object to the word being used in any cruel or mean context.

Being on the opposite side of a door is the same outcome whether you end up slamming it or pulling it closed. As members in this broader society, walk through some of those doors and talk to as many people as you can, speak to as many people as you can, and forgive as many people as you can for the missteps, misunderstandings, miscommunications, mishaps, and mistakes they have and will make with you as you embark on your own personal journey of building community by bridging your own communication gaps.

Now that we've talked about all of this Stuff, I need to say this—I do not want to live the rest of my life interpreting everything through a color-coded lens. Meaning, I do not want to have every unpleasant personal encounter, observation, statement, comment, remark, incident, or situation presented to me framed by a race perspective. I want to be able to believe that some things genuinely happen to me because as some say, "It is what it is." I don't want to always jump to the conclusion that each unpleasant encounter, observation, statement, comment, remark, incident, or situation presented was based on race first. So, while I know it may be hard, try not to link your everyday happenstance to some characteristic, but to the notion that sometimes Stuff is going to happen to you regardless, because some people are either ignorant or simply "acting stupidly" as President Obama so eloquently put it.

It is unreasonable to expect us to live in a society where there are legitimate gender and cultural differences and expect those differences and cultures not to collide intentionally or otherwise. You will eventually bump into something. As a broader culture, we are going to engage with or have conflict with people who are on the opposite side of the group we have an affinity with or opposing opinion about at some point in our lives, be it the workplace, social setting, or family. Now, whether that is opposite your race, gender, orientation, age, religion, ability, or veteran status, just because you are on the opposite side from another person doesn't mean it is those differences that are the basis of why the parties may be sparring or engaged in conflict. Real inclusion is not the absence of conflict, but the presence of social justice.

So as leaders and other professionals in the workplace, if someone brings an issue to you, address it. If someone admits to engaging in inappropriate behavior, address it. If you observe inappropriate behaviors, address it. Allow people to make mistakes with you. Allow supervisors and managers to err on the side of poor judgment. Allow colleagues to work through their own Scuff sometimes without interference. Allow time to heal the mistakes, missteps, miscommunications, misunderstandings, and mishaps created through cultural ignorance versus assumptions around intent.

As much as we desire and strive to put our best self forward, we have all been affected by personal bias, negative imagery, and stereotyping. I caution that we not be fooled on this journey because each of us is going to step on something. No one is exempt. The journey we take toward this place called "cultural competency" by building community and bridging communication gaps is not always paved, mapped out, or without pitfalls; however, it can be enriching and every step forward is worth the risk.

Epilogue

During my tenure in a leadership role as an official officer in the corporate sector, it was incumbent upon me to compel the leadership team to right the wrongs by addressing and correcting situations that were either unfair, unjust, or not in compliance with the organization's policies and procedures or federal, state, and local laws. Such a predicament is not always met with popularity and this caused me to experience job burnout. In seeking a change of venue, I began looking for opportunities that would replenish the soul because I grew tired and weary of being the solution to other people's problems and issues—the "fix it" person of bad behaviors and issues of incivility.

However, I realized that twenty-plus years performing in leadership- and compliance-related roles created the template and framework for the person I became—a seeker of justice, equality, and civil liberties for all mankind; a champion of causes because it was the right thing to do; and a spokesperson on unpopular issues in the face of political correctness. The little voice inside my head stopped telling me what I wanted to be when I grew up. I had come to understand my meaning in this life—sorting through the messy mishaps of bad behaviors. While this work has had its share of roadblocks and has been mentally and emotionally taxing and stressful, I have come to truly love this work. I was forced to listen to the voice of vocation as it was shaping my true calling. Since I was unable to get out of it, I decided to get into it. I am not sure when it happened, but somewhere along this journey I made a conscious decision to make compliance my life's work as a professional.

As I reflect on Parker J. Palmer's book *Let Your Life Speak*, I am now able to summon up the visible "detour" or "road closed" signs evident in my path that led me to the place that I am to-day—my "true calling." I grew up as a protector and a champion of meek, timid, and mild-mannered individuals who were either unable or unwilling to speak up or stand up for themselves in the face of a bully from words or from force.

Early in my career and prior to my entrée into the compliance arena, I recall two guys (senior-level managers) publicly bashing a female rep as we awaited her arrival to a meeting. They were unmerciful in the barrage of descriptors they used in reference to her looks, appearance, level of competence, and the like. When one of them called her ugly, I could no longer contain myself or have them think that I agreed with their assessment of this wom-an or that it was okay to bash her in my presence. I was also of the mindset that if they would talk about her publicly in that manner, I couldn't imagine what they would be saying about me if I wasn't in the room. I decided at that moment that they went too far and needed a dose of what they were doling out, because I was sick of them. First of all, the rep was by no means ugly, but rather a very attractive, petite, and well-dressed young lady. While I can-not recall everything I said to them, what I do recall is that one guy stopped speaking to me. What overgrown man calls a col-league ugly? Who does that? At that point in my career, while I was too young and naive to care what came out of my mouth, I was astute enough to know how to articulate it.

Even as a young person, my tolerance of incivility, injustices, and just plain rude behavior was always met with resistance from some workplace bully. One of the most compelling quotes from Palmer's book for me is "If you can't get out of it, get into it." While I at times comment that I still don't know what I want to be when I grow up—I believe that I have finally arrived. My spiritual, physical, emotional, and professional growth has led me to this space in time—a champion of the people around issues of civility, discrimination, equity, justice, and just plain old Scuuff.

References

American Democracy Project: Civic Engagement. Indiana University Purdue University at Indianapolis <http://life.iupui.edu/osi/civic-engagement/political/dp.html>

The American Heritage Dictionary of the English Language, 4th Ed. Boston, Houghton Mifflin Company, 2009.

The American Heritage Dictionary of Idioms by Christine Ammer. Houghton Mifflin Company, n.d. Dictionary.com <http://dictionary.reference.com/-browse/stuff> 14 Mar. 2013

Biber, Douglas. Dimensions of Register Variation: A Cross-Linguistic Comparison. Cambridge University Press, 1995.

Brown, James D. Rev. "What Exactly is Civil Discourse Today?" Review of In Defense of Civility: How Religion Can Unite America on Seven Moral Issues that Divide Us, by James Calvin Davis. Westminster: John Knox Press (2010).

Burgess, Heidi. "Negotiation Strategies." Beyond Intractability. Boulder: University of Colorado. Jan. 2004. <http://www.beyondintractability.org/bi-essay/negotiation-strategies>

Chappell, Bill. "Penn State Abuse Scandal: A Guide and Timeline." NPR. 21 Jun. 2012. <http://www.npr.org/2011/11/08/142111804/penn-state-abuse-scandal-a-guide-and-timeline> 16 Aug. 2013

Civility Project <http://www.harvestmoon.coop/forms/nine_rules.pdf>

Collins English Dictionary—Complete and Unabridged 10th Edition. Dictionary.com, n.d. <http://dictionary.-reference.com/browse/stuff> 14 Mar. 2013

Collins English Dictionary—Complete and Unabridged 6th Edition. HarperCollins Publishers, 2003.

Collins Thesaurus of the English Language—Complete and Unabridged 2nd Edition. HarperCollins Publishers, 2002.

Davis, Steve. "Five Ways to Facilitate Group Conversations." Unpublished article. <http://www.hodu.com/facilitate.shtml>

DeAngelis, Tori. "Unmasking 'Racial Micro Aggressions.'" American Psychological Association 40.2 (Feb. 2009): 42 <http://www. apa.org/monitor/2009/02/microaggression.aspx>

Definitions.net. STANDS4 LLC. 2013 <http://www.definitions. net/-definition/stuff> 14 Mar. 2013

Delgado, Richard and Jean Stefancic. Critical Race Theory. 2nd Ed., NYU Press, 9 Jan. 2012.

Dictionary.com <http://dictionary.reference.com/-browse/stuff> 14 Mar. 2013

The Dynamics of the Communication." Benchmark Institute n.d. <http://www.benchmarkinstitute.org/t_by_t/communica-tion/dynamics.htm>

Elliott, Phillip. "Harry Reid 'Negro' Comment: Reid Apologizes For 'No Negro Dialect' Comment." Huffington Post Politics. 9 Jan. 2010 <http://www.huffingtonpost.com/-2010/01/09/harry-reid-negro-comment-_n_417406.html>

Encarta® World English Dictionary. N. Am. Ed. 2009. Microsoft Corporation by Bloomsbury Publishing. 14 Mar. 2013

Fabian, Jordan. "Lawyer Files Lawsuit Against Obama Administration for Health Deal Records." The Hill_E² Wire (2009) 2 Jan. 2011 <http://thehill.com/blogs/e2-wire>

Gergen, Kenneth J. Social Construction in Context. (pp. 71-75). Sage. 25 May 2001.

Gudykunst, William B. Bridging Differences: Effective Intergroup Communication. 4th Ed. Los Angeles: Sage, 2004.

Gwilliam, Gary. Stella Liebeck: the Facts and Myths Surrounding the "Hot Coffee" Case. Online posting at Gwilliam Ivary Chiosso Cavalli and Brewer 15 Jul. 2011. <http://-gwilliamlawfirm. com/stella-liebeck-the-facts-and-myths-surrounding-the-hot-coffee-case/> 14 Mar. 2013

Heathfield, Susan M. "Top 10 Principles of Employee Empowerment, Empower Employees—Right—To Ensure Success and Progress." About.com. tp/empowerment.htm>

Hersey, Paul, Kenneth H. Blanchard, and Dewey E. Johnson. Management of Organizational Behavior: Leading Human Resources. 8th Ed. Prentice-Hall. Sept. 2000

Jake, A. L. and Al Reum. "American Indian Identity—Tea Parties and OutKast." (Ch. 5, About the 2004 Grammy's Performance). 2004

Kent, Julie. "Lawsuit Filed Against Obama Claims He's Not Eligible for the Presidency." Cleveland Leader 8 Aug. 2008

Kouzes, James M. and Posner, Barry Z. The Leadership Challenge. 3rd Ed. Jossey-Bass. 7 Aug. 2002.

Lovelace, Barry and Louise Menlo as About U. "Your Behavioral DNA without a Swab." Teaching Community: Where Teachers Meet and Learn. 8 Jun. 2009 <http://-teaching.monster.com/ education/articles/8533-your-behavioral-dna-without-a-swab->

Maiese, Michelle. "Negotiation." *Beyond Intractability*. Boulder: University of Colorado. Oct. 2003. <http://www.beyondin-tractability.org/bi-essay/negotiation>

Neal, Lisa M. and John Frazee. "Getting the Most Out of a Facilitated Conversation." University of Colorado 9 Feb. 2010 <http://www.ucdenver.edu/about/-departments/Ombuds Office/Documents/Tips for Getting the Most Out of a Facilitated Conversation.doc>

Pearson, Michael. "The Petraeus Affair: A Lot More Than Sex." CNN. 14 Nov. 2012. <http://www.cnn.com/2012/11/12/us/ petraeus-cia-resignation/>

Program on Intergroup Dialogue, College of Literature, Science, and the Arts, University of Michigan. <www.igr.umich.edu>

"The *Real* Facts About the McDonald's Lawsuit Coffee Case." HURT911.org <http://-www.hurt911.org/mcdonalds.html>

Sergiovanni, Thomas J., *et al.* Education Governance and

Administration. "The development of thought in educational administration." (Ch. 5, pp. 110-145). Boston: Allyn & Bacon. 1 Jun. 1998.

Serpe, Gina. "Arnold Schwarzenegger and Housekeeper Mistress: Timeline of a Scandal." E Online 18 May 2011.

Turkle, Sherry. Alone Together: Why We Expect More from Technology and Less from Each Other. New York: Basic, 2011.

WordNet 1.7.1. Princeton University. 2001 <http://wordnet.princeton.edu/>

WordNet 3.0. Farlex clipart collection. Princeton, Farlex, Inc. 2003-2008

Appendix A

Glossary of Terms

The following glossary provides clarification or an explanation related to language in the context of equal opportunity as used by the EEOC and OCR, EEO/AA professionals, and human resources practitioners.

Administrative Closure—is a charge (complaint or allegation) closed for administrative reasons, which includes: failure to locate charging party, charging party failed to respond to EEOC communications, charging party refused to accept full relief, closed due to the outcome of related litigation which establishes a precedent that makes further processing of the charge futile, charging party requests withdrawal of a charge without receiving benefits or having resolved the issue, no statutory jurisdiction.

Adverse Impact—unintentional and applies to a protected group rather than an individual. In the context of employment, refers to employment practices that appear neutral, but have a discriminatory effect on a protected group. It occurs when a decision, practice, or policy has a disproportionately negative effect on a protected group.

Allegation—unproven assertion; an assertion, especially relating to wrongdoing or misconduct on somebody's part, that has yet to be proved or supported by evidence.

Affirmative Action—the notion is to take race, ethnicity, or sex into consideration in an attempt to promote equal opportunity or increase ethnic or other forms of diversity in education and employment. The focus of such policies ranges from employment and education to public contracting and health programs. The impetus toward affirmative action is twofold. First, to maximize diversity in all levels of society, along with its presumed benefits; and second, to redress perceived disadvantages due to overt, institutional, or involuntary discrimination. While opponents argue that it promotes reverse discrimination (adversely impacts other groups), real affirmative action requires outreach that involves recruiting, training, and development actions aimed at increasing the representation of women and minorities who are qualified to meet future employment needs and who are academically accomplished to enroll in some of the top higher education institutions that pass admissions testing. Affirmative action is not about hard goals (how many); it's taking affirmative steps (good faith efforts) to increase the diversity that would not otherwise exist in employment and education.

Bullying—the generic label "bullying" applies to several forms of physical and psychological abuse having at least two major traits in common: 1) bullies select victims unlikely to defend themselves effectively; and 2) bullying is a recurring or protracted ordeal. Bullying is no longer a term referring only to schoolyard taunts and assaults, but is now fully integrated into the vocabulary of workplace harassment. Victims of bullies in the workplace are usually inferior in rank or seniority to their perpetrators (a large majority of bullies are bosses). For example, workplace bullies snub their victims, fail to share important information with them, set them up for failure, belittle victim efforts, take credit for their work, blame them for the mistakes of others, lie to them, abuse them verbally or physically, pass them over for promotion, or threaten them with dismissal. Bullied workers often believe that quitting is the only way out.

Code-switching—performs several functions to announce specific identities, create certain meanings, and facilitate particular interpersonal relationships. More specifically, people may use code-switching to hide fluency or memory problems in the second language; code-switching is used to mark switching from informal situations (using native languages) to formal situations (using second language); code-switching is used to exert control, especially between parents and children; and code-switching is used to align speakers with others in specific situations (e.g., defining oneself as a member of an ethnic group).

Communication—is the activity of conveying information through the exchange of thoughts, messages, or information as by speech, visuals, signals, writing, or behavior. It requires a sender, a message, and a recipient, although the receiver need not be present or aware of the sender's intent to communicate at the time of communication; thus communication can occur across vast distances in time and space.

Complaining Party—means the commission, the attorney general, a person or organization who may bring an action or proceeding—the party who makes the complaint in a legal action or proceeding is often referred to as the "complainant."

Complaint—an allegation of discrimination and/or harassment based on race, color, ethnicity, national origin or ancestry, sex (including sexual harassment), sexual orientation, age, disability status, religion, veteran status, or marital status or a retaliation complaint that stems from the filing of a complaint alleging such discrimination and/or harassment in violation of an organization's policy. The allegation may be made by any member of an organization's community (employee, student, staff member, faculty, donor), or by any other person who has been subjected to such discriminatory conduct by a member of the organization's community, or has been subjected to discriminatory treatment on property owned or operated by the organization or entity.

Compliance—is good faith efforts, not hard goals that fly in the face of its intended purpose. The intent of the law is to ensure that equal opportunity in education as well as in employment does not result in disparate treatment (intentional discrimination) or disparate impact (unintentional discrimination).

Demonstrates—means meets the burdens of production and persuasion.

Discrimination—consists of treating individuals or specific groups of people differently. It is illegal to discriminate against someone on the basis of race, color, religion, national origin, sex, age, pregnancy, disability, veteran status, or genetic information. The law also makes it illegal to retaliate against a person because the person complained about discrimination, filed a charge of discrimination, or participated in an employment discrimination investigation or lawsuit. The law also requires that employers reasonably accommodate applicants' and employees' sincerely held religious practices, unless doing so would impose an undue hardship on the operation of the employer's business.

Disparate Impact—is not intentional discrimination, but actions that adversely affect protected groups who have been historically underrepresented.

Disparate Treatment—intentional discrimination in the context of employment refers to when a person is treated differently from others. The different treatment is based on one or more of the protected characteristics, and the different treatment is intentional.

Employee—means an individual employed by an employer, except that the term "employee" shall not include any person elected to public office in any state or political subdivision of any state by the qualified voters thereof, or any person chosen by such officer to be on such officer's personal staff, or an appointee on the policy-making level or an immediate adviser with respect to the exercise of the constitutional or legal powers of the office. The exemption set forth in the preceding sentence shall not include employees subject to the civil service laws of a state government, governmental agency, or political subdivision. With respect to employment in a foreign country, such term includes an individual who is a citizen of the United States.

Harassment—is a form of discrimination. Harassment is unwelcome conduct that is based on race, color, religion, sex (including pregnancy), national origin, age (forty or older), disability, or genetic information. Harassment becomes unlawful where 1) enduring the offensive conduct becomes a condition of continued employment, or 2) the conduct is severe or pervasive enough to create a work environment that a reasonable person would consider intimidating, hostile, or abusive. Anti-discrimination laws also prohibit harassment against individuals in retaliation for filing a discrimination charge, testifying, or participating in any way in an investigation, proceeding, or lawsuit under these laws; or opposing employment practices that they reasonably believe discriminate against individuals, in violation of these laws.

Although the law doesn't prohibit simple teasing, offhand comments, or isolated incidents that are not very serious, petty slights and annoyances (unless extremely serious) will not rise to the level of illegality. To be unlawful, the conduct must create a work environment that would be intimidating, so frequent, or severe that it creates a hostile or offensive work environment to reasonable people; or when it results in an adverse employment decision (such as the victim being fired or demoted).

Offensive conduct may include, but is not limited to, offensive jokes, slurs, epithets or name calling, physical assaults or threats, intimidation, ridicule or mockery, insults or putdowns, offensive objects or pictures, and interference with work performance. Harassment can occur in a variety of circumstances, including, but not limited to, the following:

The harasser can be the victim's supervisor, a supervisor in another area, an agent of the employer, a co-worker, or a non-employee such as a client or customer. The victim does not have to be the person harassed, but can be anyone affected by the offensive conduct. Unlawful harassment may occur without economic injury to, or discharge of, the victim.

Sexual harassment—is a form of illegal harassment that includes inappropriate behaviors ranging from unwelcome sexual advances, requests for sexual favors, and other verbal or physical harassment of a sexual nature for persons of either gender, including same-sex harassment. Harassment does not have to be of a sexual nature, and can include offensive remarks about a person's sex. For example, it is illegal to harass a woman by making offensive comments about women in general.

Intervention—is where the EEOC joins a lawsuit that has been filed by a private plaintiff.

Mediation—is an informal and confidential way for people to resolve disputes with the help of a neutral mediator who is trained to help people discuss their differences. The mediator does not decide who is right or wrong or issue a decision. Instead, the mediator helps the parties work out their own solutions to problems.

Merit Resolutions—charges with outcomes favorable to charging parties and/or charges with meritorious allegations. These include negotiated settlements, withdrawals with benefits, successful conciliations, and unsuccessful conciliations.

Merits Suits—include direct suits and interventions alleging violations of the substantive provisions of the statutes enforced by the EEOC and suits to enforce administrative settlements.

Micro-aggression—micro-aggression is defined as actions or inactions by individuals that perpetuate the status quo of racism, homophobia, sexism, and xenophobia. Micro-aggressions are the everyday verbal, nonverbal, and environmental slights, snubs, or insults, whether intentional or unintentional, which communicate hostile, derogatory, or negative messages to target persons based solely on their race, ethnicity, sex, sexual orientation, religion, ability, and so on. Repeated micro-aggression and micro-insults wear down blacks. For example, when a white child and a black child enter a store, guards follow the black child; and when a black person sits in first class, the flight attendants ask if they are in the right place. Micro-aggressions are those many sudden, stunning, or dispiriting transactions that mar the days of women and people of color. Like water dripping on sandstone, they can be thought of as small acts of sexism, racism, or other "isms."

Micro-assaults—conscious and intentional actions or slurs, such as using racial epithets, displaying swastikas, or deliberately serving a white person before a person of color in a restaurant.

Micro-inequity—a micro-inequity is defined as a subtle message, sometimes subconscious, that devalues, discourages, and ultimately impairs performance in the workplace. These messages can take the shape of looks, gestures, or even tones. The cumulative effect of micro-inequities often leads to damaged self-esteem and, eventually, withdrawal from co-workers in the office.

Micro-insults—verbal and nonverbal communications that subtly convey rudeness and insensitivity and demean a person's racial heritage or identity. An example is an employee who asks a colleague of color how she got her job, implying she may have landed it through an affirmative action or quota system.

Micro-invalidations—communications that subtly exclude, negate, or nullify the thoughts, feelings, or experiential reality of a person of color. For instance, white people often ask Asian-Americans where they were born, conveying the message that they are perpetual foreigners in their own land.

Miscommunication—to communicate mistakenly, unclearly, or inadequately.

Mishap—an unfortunate accident, bad luck.

Misstep—a wrong step, fault, transgression, lapse, or indiscretion—an error or slip in conduct; faux pas.

Misunderstanding—a failure to understand or interpret correctly the words or behavior of; to take words or statements in the wrong sense; or mistake as to meaning or intent.

No Reasonable Cause—EEOC's determination of no reasonable cause to believe that discrimination occurred based upon the evidence obtained during the investigation. The charging party may exercise the right to bring private court action.

Reasonable Cause—EEOC's determination of reasonable cause to believe that discrimination occurred based upon the evidence obtained during the investigation. Reasonable cause determinations are generally followed by efforts to conciliate the discriminatory issues which gave rise to the initial charge.

Religion—includes all aspects of religious observance and practice, as well as belief, unless an employer can demonstrate that they are unable to reasonably accommodate an employee's or prospective employee's religious observance or practice without undue hardship on the operation of the employer's business.

Respondent—means an employer, employment agency, labor organization, joint labor management committee controlling apprenticeship, or other training or retraining program, including an on-the-job training program, or Federal entity. The party responding to the complaint in a legal action or proceeding is often referred to as the "respondent."

Settlements (Negotiated)—charges settled with benefits to the charging party as warranted by evidence of record. The Indiana Civil Rights Commission is one of nine FEPA's (Fair Employment Practices Agency) working in collaboration with the EEOC to build upon a mutual goal of eradicating discrimination in the workplaces of America. In such cases, EEOC and/or a FEPA is a party to the settlement agreement between the charging party and the respondent (an employer, union, or other entity covered by EEOC-enforced statutes).

Subpoena Enforcement Actions—are filed during the course of the investigation of a charge of discrimination where the respondent refuses to provide information relevant to the charge.

Successful Conciliation—charge with reasonable cause determination closed after successful conciliation. Successful conciliations result in substantial relief to the charging party and all others adversely affected by the discrimination.

Suits to Enforce Administrative Settlements—involve a respondent's breach of an agreement with the EEOC to settle a charge during the administrative process.

Unsuccessful Conciliation—charge with reasonable cause determination closed after efforts to conciliate the charge are unsuccessful. Pursuant to commission policy, the field office will close the charge and review it for litigation consideration.

Withdrawal with Benefits—a charge is withdrawn by charging party upon receipt of desired benefits. The withdrawal may take place after a settlement or after the respondent grants the appropriate benefit to the charging party.

Appendix B

Enforcement Agency Resources

Equal Employment Opportunity Commission
Homepage—http://www.eeoc.gov/

Filing a charge of discrimination
http://www.eeoc.gov/employees/charge.cfm

Filing a lawsuit
http://www.eeoc.gov/employees/lawsuit.cfm

Office of Civil Rights
Homepage—
http://www.ed.gov/about/offices/list/ocr/index.html

Office of Federal Contract Compliance Programs
Homepage—http://www.dol.gov/OFCCP/index.htm

Appendix C

Tips for Getting the Most Out of a Facilitated Conversation

"We cannot solve problems by using the same kind of thinking we used when we created them." —attributed to Albert Einstein

Test Assumptions

Human beings are meaning-making creatures. Often, however, we make meaning without all the facts in hand. We leap from hearing someone make a comment to making judgments about his or her character and integrity in a matter of a second or two—and without conscious thought. Once you become aware of this process, you can catch yourself before making the leap and instead ask for more information or clarification.

Share Relevant Information and Your Reasoning

When you are speaking, you can help the other party avoid making unwarranted assumptions and leaping to unfounded conclusions by sharing your reasoning as well as the information behind your reasoning. As a listener, when you wonder why the other party is saying something, that's your cue to ask a question.

Use Specific Examples

Making broad generalizations can contribute to misunderstanding and provoke defensiveness. Using specific examples ensures that relevant information is shared and understood.

Use "I" Statements, Not "You" Statements

"You intimidated me" is likely to provoke a defensive response. "I felt intimidated when I perceived that you were becoming angry in the department meeting" provides valid information and context rather than making judgments. It can start a conversation rather than an argument.

Agree on What Important Words Mean

A remarkably common source of misunderstanding and conflict is using words without shared understanding of their meaning. When you're using a word that's important to the conversation, don't assume that the other party shares your understanding of its meaning. Explain what you mean.

Stay Curious

All of the tips above come down to this: If you can stay curious in the conversation, you will avoid making premature judgments about the conflict or the other party. Staying curious creates an opportunity for learning for both parties. It also helps repair and strengthen your relationships. In the middle of a difficult conversation, it can be tough to stay open to new information. But it's essential to the process.

Exercise Compassion

For the purpose of having a fruitful conversation, temporarily suspend your judgments toward others—and yourself, too. Recognize that few if any conflicts arise without *both* parties contributing in some way to the conflict. That doesn't make the other person—or you—a bad person, only human. A facilitated conversation offers an opportunity to move beyond simple judgments of good and bad toward greater insight into the nature and meaning of the conflict, how it arose, and how it can be resolved in a way that strengthens both parties and their relationship

Source: University of Colorado Denver Ombuds Office
www.ucdenver.edu/about/departments/OmbudsOffice/...
DOCfile

Ten Principles of Employee Empowerment

1. Demonstrate that you value people through your words and deeds.
2. Share your leadership vision with employees by helping them feel they are a part of something bigger than themselves.
3. Share the most important goals and direction for your team and make sure the progress on those goals is measurable and observable.
4. Trust that people will do the right thing and make the right decisions and choices, even if those decisions are not exactly what you would do.
5. Provide information for decision making and make sure people have what they need to make an informed decision.
6. Delegate authority and impact opportunities, not just more work. Involve people in the important meetings, committee memberships that impact the organization, and projects that people and customers notice.
7. Provide frequent feedback so people know how they're doing.
8. Solve problems and do not pinpoint problem people when problems arise. Ask what's wrong that caused people to fail versus what's wrong with the people.
9. Listen to learn and ask questions to provide guidance. Provide a space in which people will communicate by listening to them and asking them questions. Guide by asking questions, not by telling grown people what to do.

10. Help employees feel rewarded and recognized for empowered behavior—when employees feel unappreciated, underpaid, under-titled, and undervalued, don't expect results. For successful employee empowerment to occur, some form of recognition must be evident.

Source: Susan M. Heathfield, Human Resources Guide, About.com, The Top 10 Principles of Employee Empowerment. http://humanresources.about.com/od/managementandleadership/tp/empowerment.htm

CPSIA information can be obtained at www.ICGtesting.com
Printed in the USA
LVIW01n0347070715
445192LV00002B/4